GRIEF'S ABYSS

FINDING YOUR PATHWAY TO PEACE

BY ANNE E. DEBUTTE

Copyright © 2015 Anne E. DeButte. All rights reserved. No portion of this book may be reproduced mechanically, electronically, or by any other means, including photocopying, without written permission of the publisher. It is illegal to copy this book, post it to a website, or distribute it by any other means without permission from the publisher.

Love Your Life Publishing
Wilmington, DE
www.loveyourlifepublishing.com

ISBN: 978-1-934509-81-4
Library of Congress Control Number: 2014921315
Printed in the United States of America
First Printing 2015
Cover design by 2FacedDesign.com

This book is designed to provide information on grief only. This information is provided and sold with the knowledge that the publisher and author do not offer any legal or other professional advice. In the case of a need for any such expertise consult with the appropriate professional. This book does not contain all information available on the subject. This book has not been created to be specific to any individual's or organizations' situation or needs. Every effort has been made to make this book as accurate as possible. This book is intended only to educate and entertain. The author and publisher shall have no liability or responsibility to any person or entity regarding any loss or damage incurred, or alleged to have incurred, directly or indirectly, by the information contained in this book. You hereby agree to be bound by this disclaimer or you may return this book within the guarantee time period for a full refund.

ADVANCE PRAISE FOR GRIEF'S ABYSS

"Grief isn't about a broken head, but a broken heart. Anne's book will help you find forgiveness and healing, as she did. I highly recommend Anne — both her book and her coaching are delightful." - Aurora Winter, author of Grief Relief in 30 Minutes

"This book offers hope with a plan. It does a comprehensive job of touching on the many types of loss, and offers helpful suggestions for coping. I would recommend this to anyone who is grieving or knows someone who is grieving for the loss of a loved one. A well-written book about a very difficult subject." - Judy O'Beirn, Creator and co-author of international bestselling book Unwavering Strength

"*Grief's Abyss* is a book that everyone who is going through the grieving process should read. The book will bring you comfort and is written with great compassion. Anne Debutte does an amazing job helping the reader come to terms with their loss." - Lori Kay, Ph.D., Psychologist, Author

"This book will (at the very least) help in understanding the natural phenomenon of grief following the loss of a loved one. It has the potential to do much more – it may provide direction out of *Grief's Abyss* and into a new, healthy reality beyond loss." - Jason R. Pantarotto MD FRCPC

"This is a book that will become a friend to its reader-- a practical and tender guide through the journey of grief." - Sharae Buskirk, Hospice Bereavement Care Coordinator

"*Grief's Abyss* is Anne's intensely personal and bone-honest story. With permission to welcome the full range of feelings associated with grief, she guides us like a loving older sister through the loss of a loved one. For anyone struggling with how to deal with heart-break, this book is a source of gentle wisdom." -Andrea Mathieson, Midlife Midwife

"**Grief's Abyss** is a thoughtfully written guide to navigating a loss. Anne's warmth and compassion wraps you with loving and supportive advice on how to crawl out of the well of sadness when experiencing the loss of a loved one. A must-read for anyone grieving the loss of a loved one." -Kristen Sutich, Personal Coach

"Anne DeButte's journey from *Grief's Abyss* to a renewal of happiness and peace will be a positive help for all us all when faced with the inevitable grief at the loss of a loved one. Highly recommended." ~ **Dr Barry L. Whitney, University of Windsor (retired)**

"This is brilliant. It is by far the best I have read on grief. Bravo. Easy to read, digest and brings in the energy /archetype of HOPE." ~ **Lilly White, www.powerupyourlife.ca**

"*Grief's Abyss is* great resource for what each and every one of us will face in our lives or have been through many times. Having been in the nursing profession for 50 yrs. now, we who provide our services are often in the position to comfort and provide counselling at the very time of loss of a loved one. *Grief's Abyss* would have been most welcomed to me many years ago when I lost family members. I recommend it highly." ~ **Angela G. Bertrend, Psychiatric Nurse, Royal Ottawa Mental Health Group**

"I am moved and touched by Anne's personal story of loss and grief. She uses her own deeply personal experience to gently guide the reader through the grief and loss journey. I particularly appreciate the life-giving reflection questions that set me on a new path of healing, hope and wholeness." ~ **Lillas Marie Hatala, MCEd., CHRP, CMC Integrative Leadership International Ltd. Calgary, AB Canada**

"Grief's Abyss will be an immediate comfort to anyone who is experiencing grief. The reader will feel like they are not alone, they are understood, and there is a path for finding their way out of grief." ~ **Babette Zschiegner, Author of Traveling with your Autistic Child: 76 Tips for Joyful Family Adventures**

"With this courageous book, Anne DeButte gives us a sort of road map through the intense emotions of grief. Through it we understand how normal it is to experience the disorientation and altered states we encounter when loved ones die, plus some good pointers to help us through the unfamiliar terrain." ~ **Dhyanis Carniglia, Certified "From Heartbreak to Happiness®" Grief Coach**

"Anne is amazingly connected with her thoughts and emotions. She has a gift for knowing what's happening on the inside and has a way of articulating it in a way that not many people can. It is through this gift that she is able to describe her own journey through grief and in doing so, will help others connect with what they are truly thinking and feeling as they navigate their way out of *Grief's Abyss*." ~ **Bradley Preston, Engineering student, University of Victoria, BC**

"The fact that Anne herself has walked the road of grief and has now found peace, gives her the authentic ability to help the reader in their own journey." ~ **Jayne Blumenthal, Business Strategist and Success Mindset Mentor**

"As a baby boomer, who has not yet had to cope with the loss of either parent, I have given thought as to what my reactions might and will be, and how I will cope losing two individuals who have the "rocks of support" in my life. How will I handle my grief and support my children and my siblings in their grief as well? I also like to have a map for journeys and hope that *Grief's Abyss* can be a resource and guide for me in the destination of the journey of grief. The messages are very reassuring." ~ **Sue McCutcheon, RN, COHN©**

"Anne has a wonderful way of painting images with words. Her writing style draws you in and slows you down. As I read the chapters in this book I was impressed with the images and softness of the words, clearly written by someone who has "been there". This is a book that allows someone who is grieving to know that others have walked the way before and, while not offering to "fix" things, can offer guidance on the road to be travelled through grief towards healing and wholeness. I would certainly add this book to my book shelves and into my "tool kit" as I walk alongside those who grieve. I would happily suggest it as a resource and use it as a guide for conversations.

Particularly helpful are the short questions at the end of the chapters. Too often those who are grieving feel helpless and these questions for reflection allow the reader to dig into their own well of resourcefulness and spirit leading to wholeness. " - **Rev. Elaine Beattie**

CONTENTS

13 **Introduction**

17 Chapter 1
    Welcome to Grief's Abyss

25 Chapter 2
    Making Sense of Emotions

37 Chapter 3
    Candle in the Darkness

47 Chapter 4
    Living in Two Worlds

59 Chapter 5
    Making Sense of Loss

71 Chapter 6
    Faith is Either Lost or Strengthened

83 Chapter 7
    Telling Your Story and Being Supported

95 Chapter 8
    Seasons of Grief

107 Chapter 9
    Needs of Grief for Healing

119 Chapter 10
    Grief's Gifts

129 Chapter 11
    Acknowledging and Forgiving

139 Chapter 12
    Finding Hope and Joy

150 **Recommended Resources**

155 **Acknowledgements**

157 **About the Author**

In loving memory of Arthur Purdon,
whose death inspired me to write

and Beth Purdon, whose support and love
allowed me to follow my dreams.

THE JOURNEY

The river of life flows through us all
Then when a death occurs, we get to fall
into Grief's Abyss, a dark unfamiliar place
Down into the valley where we all must face
How to cope with all the changes
when the familiar landscape rearranges
Gone are the roads and highways once travelled
as our lives become unravelled

We've taken a wrong turn;
we're not meant to be here
We look around us and go into fear
as our compass resets and
the road on the map shows
we must follow this path along
where the river flows
Through a forest of Grief, this pathway we see
widens and intersects—which to take
so we'll be free?
One road leads to the flatlands,
which go on for miles
there is nothing of interest it seems that will
bring back smiles

The other has a roundabout with
three roads just around a bend
Guilt, anger and acceptance; oh,
when will this journey end
Choose one, for the only way through
is to openly mourn
So many people have traveled here long
before you were born
Each has found his or her own way out and
you will too

You will leave this land behind to face life anew
The climb back is steep; let me lead the way
I know you doubt, "How does she know?"
I hear you say

For I have traveled through here some time ago
I got to claim my prize, Grief's Gifts and
I'm now in life's flow
A review of your journey will show
where you've been
glimpses of your growth, goals and
purpose all seen
We are all here to welcome you back for
we know you are worthy
You've been gone for a while on your own
a Hero's journey
Whenever we get back into the river of life
that flows through us all,
We'll take comfort—we have our map and
are ready if we fall
into Grief's Abyss for we know

The Wheels of Samsara turn;
the cycle of life continues

Anne E. DeButte

INTRODUCTION

My dad was the painter in the family. He taught my sister and I to appreciate nature, wildlife, a river—just about anything to him was a potential subject. Unfortunately, at the time, we did not appreciate his fine eye, although we loved nature and being outdoors. Our eyes saw the delights of play and not through the lens of a painter.

The gift that my dad did give me, however, was to see the beauty in nature so I could paint it with words. Just like an artist hones his painting skills, I, too, am honing my skills to paint with words. We never think about the death of our parents. They have been there forever; they will always be there for us. Our landscape changes when one is taken from us. It has been more than two years since my father died, but his gifts to me continue to grow. They have lain dormant, like compost decaying, which eventually turns into rich fertile soil. My desire to write, timid at first, just like newly planted seeds, has started to root and grow. The words to describe what I want to say get stuck and hang back in fear, but when they do come forth, I delight in their creation. But I have gotten ahead of myself and need to slowly go back to when it began, this desire of mine.

It was in those first months of grief that I was tormented by emotions, unable to think or work. Everything was such an effort, even the simplest of tasks. I felt lost and eventually did lose myself for a time. A small seed of a thought took hold during those early days of my grief and began to grow louder and louder with each day. What I needed was a road map or perhaps a grief map. So I decided that I would write a book—a book that would assist me and others in knowing what to expect. I could guide readers and show them the way through and, eventually, out.

A map seemed like a great idea because whenever I go on a journey, I always take one along. My dad had taught me from an early age how to read road maps, another of his gifts to me. I am forever grateful because if I get lost, I can easily find my way back. It is a comfort to me to know that I have this ability and inner compass.

Due to this need of mine to keep safe and know where I am, I have a map, my compass to point me in the right direction. When my dad died, I didn't have one; my inner compass was broken and just kept spinning around. This went on for the next six months.

I recognize now that I was in the clutches of grief's watery hands. Its effects were present in everything I did or didn't do. My brain felt waterlogged. I couldn't think or function properly. My eyes from time to time would release the pressure and allow the tears to flow. My heart was drowning in the turbulent waters as it was tossed around by all the emotions ever known to humankind.

I lived in this watery land of grief and, at times, I thought I would never get out. To me, it felt like an abyss, which, according to the dictionary, describes beautifully what I was experiencing. It was deep and it took up immeasurable space; it was unfathomable and infinite; it was pure, primal chaos and it felt like hell.

However, each day some new experience—sometimes laughter, like the sun—would peep through, showing me a way out. I relied purely on instinct and intuition. This was a journey that I had to experience alone, without any external tools, and certainly with no beloved map to lend comfort.

My grief had pushed and pulled at me. It even shook me so that I would release all the things in my life that no longer mattered. The petty arguments with my father tucked away in my memory were released and washed away. After about six months, grief deemed that I had been emotionally cleansed and slowly receded from my life. I felt lighter but still dazed.

Then sunshine and blue skies beckoned me on to another part of my life. I was now in calmer waters. In fact, I had found dry land and was ready to move on with my life. Although no longer buffeted by raging waters, I remained exhausted. For me, the land of grief was bewildering because I had never been taught what was expected of me or what to expect from the experience.

Eventually, I was able to emerge from my journey in grief. It took time, introspection, support, and much self care. I emerged stronger and wiser because I'd traveled grief's many waterways and highways. It was a difficult journey and one that all of us will eventually experience.

This book is the road map that resulted from my journey through grief. May it be a blessing and comfort to you on your journey through grief as well.

To help you glean the most from this book, I've prepared some additional resources for you. You can find them at **www.reconnect-from-grief.com/readergift**.

CHAPTER I

> Grief comes in one size, extra large. If we tuck it away in the bottom drawer where it never sees the light of day, it remains exactly the same. On the other hand, if we wear it, feel it, talk about it, and share it with others, it is likely it will become faded, shrunk and worn and will simply no longer fit. When grief has served its purpose, we are able to recognize the many gifts we have gained.
>
> Dianne Arcangel

WELCOME TO GRIEF'S ABYSS

WALKING ALONG the pathway in the flow of life, just like a river flowing gently along, we never think about our lives that much when life is good. We just want more and to continue on our path, like a river. We never really know what lies ahead. Our gentle flowing river goes for miles and then suddenly drops, raging over the rocks. Tons of powerful water tumble and churn over and down, flowing until it reaches the bottom of the gorge. There, the water continues to merge into itself. Once collected and reorganized, it returns to a gentle flow. The river, upon seeing the rocks and steep drop below, doesn't retreat into fear and cling to the mountaintop. Instead, it allows itself to be drawn downward, knowing that eventually it will arrive where it is supposed to be.

Grief's Abyss

How different are we when someone we love dies? With their death, we are taken from our gently flowing lives and plunged deep into a gorge, where we spin and spin. This gorge is grief's abyss.

Grief separates us from all that we've known. It disconnects and unplugs us from the familiar and takes us to places that we are loathe to visit.

There is no comfort to be found in grief. It is about journeying, moving, constricting, and withdrawing. This journey with grief takes us down to those dark places where no one wants to go, where cobwebs abound, a place that is dark, damp, cold, unfamiliar, and full of pain.

Grief takes you here to re-examine your life, motives, and relationships ... that is, if you dare. It allows you to examine all of your accumulated losses in one swift moment. When a loved one dies, you may be shocked to find that you begin to feel deep pain, not only for the passing of your loved one, but also for lesser losses in and of your life, that which have been lying dormant, waiting to be confronted.

You get the opportunity to examine all that has been lost—the childhood hurts, regrets, and discarded parts of yourself. Grief's only request is that you follow its lead and allow the journey to unfold, much like the flowing river described earlier.

Like all good journeys, the more you know about the destination and about what you can expect from it, the less your fears will be in undertaking it. The more you know and understand about grief, the better your journey through it will be. To know that what you are experiencing is normal, and something to be expected when someone you love is taken from you, can help ease the pain. The fear of the unknown can cause greater pain and leads to the need to hold on, to try to control everything. Such behavior lends the illusion that you are keeping yourself safe. Sadly, this tactic can keep you stuck in the abyss. Know that your fears are both normal and natural, and arise in order to force you to confront and work through them. They are part of the grieving process. By facing your emotions as they arise and by allowing them to move fully through you, you will become less fearful of them. You may notice along the journey, however, that your emotions will vacillate between bursting forth and retreating. Allow them to do what they need to. Once they have been fully worked through, they will depart.

If you follow grief's lead, you will find that you can lessen the time that you spend being stuck in it. I will be sharing more of these roundabouts later in the book. Just know that this is the easiest way to start climbing out of grief's abyss so you can get reconnected with your life and feel renewed energy. You will emerge as a new you and will be able to rewrite your new life, one that is on purpose, and filled with much more joy and peace. Grief is an internal expression of what you are feeling deeply, your emotions of poignant distress.

Grief is a journey of discovery, one where the heart leads and the head follows, because we cannot think ourselves totally out of grief. Our minds want us to move on before our hearts are finished with the feelings. Grieving involves many emotions that help the person who is grieving come to terms with the loss.

> **If you truly want to grow as a person and learn, you should realize that the universe has enrolled you in the graduate program of life, called loss.**
> Elisabeth Kübler-Ross

MY GRIEF JOURNEY BEGINS

EACH JOURNEY into grief's abyss is unique and harrowing. I want to briefly share my journey with you so you can trust I have walked the same road that you are now on. I've found my peace and want to help you find yours.

This is how my journey of grief began:
> November 17 was one of the saddest days of my life; it was on this day that my father passed away. The color of my world was forever changed.

> I can't go back to yesterday because
> I was a different person then.
>
> Lewis Carroll in **Alice in Wonderland**

When someone is taken from you in death, what do you do first? The child in me wanted to be led by the hand; the responsibility felt too great. The adult in me felt frozen, unable to digest the situation and know how to proceed. I was momentarily lost.

My dad died just before I arrived at the Emergency Room. As I stood there, a million things were going through my head. Nothing made sense; my mind was spinning. Neither I nor my mother had any prior experience with death and what would follow it. In fact, I had never even attended a family funeral before because we had no relatives in Canada, where we were living.

I had worked as a nurse earlier in my life when we lived in Britain. On the ward, when a person passed away, the chaplain would come and help to take care of the families. The family members would be ushered away and given a cup of tea. This allowed the nurses to continue their duties and prepare the body. This task was carried out in quiet reverence for the person, efficiently and clinically. The body was then transported to the morgue. What happened after that, I never bothered to find out. Back then, I was in my twenties. That question didn't seem relevant or important to me. But when my father died, I wasn't one of the nurses tending to a stranger but rather the daughter of the deceased. What was my role in this situation? I didn't know; this part of my life had not yet been written. After all, it's not something that you can rehearse for.

We were asked by one of the nurses if we would like the hospital chaplain to come. At first, we said no, believing that we would be fine all by ourselves. The nurse, however, seemed to sense some hesitancy on my part and asked again. I realized that both my mom and I could benefit from outside support. I hoped Mum would find solace in the chaplain's visit as well. My parents were always very private people and never wanted to be a bother to anyone, always preferring to do things on their own. I tended to do the same. But this time, things were different. I really wanted the chaplain's guidance. I needed someone to lead me through these unfamiliar waters and take charge. How long do we stay here at the hospital? What would people think if we just left right away? We could stay, but to do what? We knew there were things we needed to do (other than just stand there and sob), but we didn't necessarily want to leave the hospital at that moment either. It was confusing and uncomfortable.

When the chaplain came and spoke to us, we found her words comforting. Our tears flowed as she softly quoted familiar scripture. Then she gently asked if we had any questions. Although I had tons of thoughts swirling in my head, I couldn't seem to get them formulated into sentences. I remained silent, secretly wishing that she would sense this and promptly take my mum and me somewhere and tell us everything we needed to know and do. We hugged and thanked her in our best stoic British manner. As soon as she left, we were right back to being alone. I looked down at Dad and held his hand. Silently, I told my dad's spirit to go toward the light. This thought gave me immense comfort; I had dabbled in Eastern philosophy for a time and this seemed the right thing to say.

At this point, the shock was wearing off and guilt was settling in. Why hadn't I been taught what to do? I felt foolish standing there. No one else approached us. The nursing staff kept its distance. I felt in limbo, trying to think of what the protocol should be for families who had experienced the sudden death of a beloved family member. Was there even such a thing?

We decided it was time to leave and said our goodbyes to Dad, although we were still hesitant to walk out the door. We felt that we were now intruding; it was, after all, the Emergency Room and the nurses had work to do. Perhaps someone else was waiting for the space ... Another 10 to 20 minutes passed, and Mum said, "I do think we should leave now." I nodded, and we turned to go.

Once again, I felt helpless and alone. Arm in arm, Mum and I silently stepped out into the daylight, each mired in our own thoughts. Although

Grief's Abyss

time had stopped for us, the rest of the world went about its business. Cars sped by. People shuffled past us. I wanted to scream aloud, "My dad just died. How can you all keep moving and act as if nothing has happened!" But I just swallowed it down and crammed it back inside. Again, I came back to my British roots, knowing it was time to practise that proverbial British stiff upper lip or better still, stay calm, carry on, and have a cup of tea!

Carry on we did. Mum and I crossed the parking lot to the car, feeling invisible to all those busy people around us. Our hearts were heavy and our lives were in disarray.

A NEW TITLE: BEREAVED

THE PERSON you loved is now deceased. You haven't had a chance to recognize that you are no longer a daughter, son, wife, husband, or parent to that person. But you are a "bereaved person." This just adds another dimension to the loss. Not knowing where you fit into society can cause further distress.

When you are bereaved, your energy levels and mental functioning diminish and, in general, everything becomes an effort. You feel as though you have to push yourself to get anything accomplished and to make it through the day. The process of grieving is taxing on your body, leaving you tired and exhausted. Thus, your thinking is often cloudy and hazy; it is hard to pull your thoughts together. Your mind wanders. It is difficult to hold yourself. Your head is just beginning to make sense of what has happened. Whatever is going on in this present moment doesn't seem to bear any resemblance to you and what you need. You are not ready to live in the present because to be fully in the moment would mean acceptance of your loss, and you are not yet ready to go there. Your mind is pulling you in that direction, but your heart is not able to fully follow.

You have picked up this book because you are looking for answers; you want to reduce the time spent in pain and heartache so you can move on to a more peaceful existence. How quickly you are able to get through the pain will depend on you and what your coping skills are. How well do you handle change? Nothing alters our lives more than the death of a loved one. When a death occurs, we realize what we can and cannot control in life. We have to face the fact that when it comes to death, we are powerless. This sense of no power is scary and awakens our primordial fears of survival. You may be scared to know what is in front of you, and that is perfectly OK too. There is a lot of information to process. Take heart knowing that this is a frightening journey for all of us because we have never been told what to expect, or prepared for the event. Everything about death has become so clinical; we have given our power away to the medical profession and to funeral directors. It is time to take some of that power back. Knowing what to expect when a loved one passes can help to eradicate the fears.

One thing you won't find in this book is a quick fix or a one-size-fits-all solution for the pain. How you think and how willing you are to accept the situation can and will help ease your suffering. If you believe that you will never get over the grief and the loss, then perhaps you are right. But if, on the other hand, you believe that you can make sense of all of this, then you are also right. We are what we think, and it is our thoughts about the future that can awaken our fears. This is good because you can never be aware of what those fears are until you see why they are coming to the surface and, if you don't bring them into the light, your fears will overtake and sabotage you. You get to choose the outcome of this journey.

REFLECTIONS

Answering these questions will help you increase your understanding of the concepts in each chapter by applying them to your own experience. You may answer the questions here in the book or in a journal that you can download from www.reconnect-from-grief.com/readergift.

1 Journal: Tell your story

There is no need to share your story with anyone else at this point. Just tell it to yourself by writing it down, crying about it, and acknowledging it. Doing so will help to get it out of your head and help remove the chaos in your mind.

2 Think about what brings you enjoyment

Make a list of three things you enjoy. Make sure you do at least one of these things every day. Grieving is hard work, and you need a break doing something that which is pleasing to you.

3 Why did you pick up this book?

Make a list of what it is you are hoping to get out of this book. This will help you to know what your needs are at the moment.

CHAPTER 2

> Life is not the way it's supposed to be.
> It's the way it is. The way you cope with
> it is what makes the difference.
>
> Virginia Satir

MAKING SENSE OF EMOTIONS

LET'S GO BACK to my story for a moment. The seven days that followed the death of my father were a whirlwind as my mum and I struggled to organize ourselves, figure out a plan for the funeral, gather family and friends, and go through the motions of being in control. We did not really know what we were doing; we both just pasted on happy faces and tried to pretend. There was no time to think ... only time to try to be strong. We would have to deal with our emotions after all these items were taken care of.

How many of us try to stay strong for others? Not wanting to upset our family and friends, we try to pull ourselves together and remain stoic for them. Ironically, we also do this for ourselves. If we were to release all of our emotions at this point, we feel certain they would overpower us.

When I did finally find myself alone after those seven days of so many events and so much activity, I was able to let go and delve into the chaos, the abyss, and the uncertainty of my emotions. I had held it together and remained strong until after the funeral. But then, my emotions broke loose and I had to deal with them.

I was sure that I didn't need anyone. I just needed some guidelines and structure. The only book I knew of about grief was The Five Stages of Grief, by Dr. Elisabeth Kübler-Ross. In it, she describes the five stages as shock, anger, bargaining, depression, and acceptance. All of these are what a person facing his or her own death is likely to experience. I was introduced to this book during my volunteer days in Palliative Care. Dr. Kübler-Ross's work, I don't believe, was ever intended to be used for the grief experienced from the death of a loved one. I only mention this because I knew of no other resource from which to draw comfort. For my own situation, I could relate to the first two stages—the shock and anger. As for the others, I just wasn't sure at this point.

I started to use her model to see if I could sort out my emotions and feelings, which were all muddled and jumbled together. Although Kübler-Ross refers to five stages of grieving, I prefer to call them all emotions and feelings. Upon reflection, I realized that I had already experienced most of these emotions and feelings during the hour after I received the first call from my mum that awful day, alerting me about Dad's situation. I have shared examples of this in the hope that it will help you better understand what you may be feeling, if you are currently experiencing grief.

Denial—Although we cannot deny there has been a death, our mind will protect us from this shock until we are ready to process what has happened.

For me, this is what I experienced when I first received the phone call at work:

"There is something wrong with Dad," Mum said. "I've called for an ambulance and for the care worker. She was supposed to show up to help me today. I will let you know more when I do."

The call left me in a panic, uncertain as to how to proceed. Should

I leave work now and go to my parents' home immediately? But, what if the ambulance already arrived and took them to the hospital? Which hospital was I to drive to? Better to stay put. Another phone call followed. This time it was from the care worker.

"Your mum has called to let us know about your dad. I am on my way and will take your mum to whatever hospital they take your dad to," she said.

I thanked her and waited by my desk for the next call. Although I tried to work, it was to no avail. I kept trying to decide what the best plan of action was. Should I alert people at work just in case? Oh, I need to let my sister know, but she is working and I'm not sure what to say to her at this point. I didn't do anything. I was paralyzed in some ways, as a million questions and thoughts were flooding my brain. A third phone call came. This time I was told which hospital to go to.

"OK, I am on my way," I said. I was still at work 15 minutes later trying to explain to everyone where I was going. "Let me drive you," a colleague said.

"No, I will be fine. Besides, I need my car because my husband is out of town." Finally I left, stepping outside and leaving the familiar behind to face the unknown.

Shock and Numbness—Mechanisms that protect the mind and numb the body; they help us to process the many thoughts and events that are occurring at the same time and overwhelming us.

It was in this state that I drove to the hospital. I was fine until I discovered that the road I normally take to the highway was closed. I panicked, finding myself unable to think of another route. I had lived there for more than 30 years and knew the city well, but suddenly, the landscape looked strange. After several turns, I found a familiar road. But then, I couldn't remember what exit to take to get to the hospital. I was losing precious minutes. "Mum will be so cross," was all I could think. My world had slowed down in some ways. I should not have been driving in this condition. Instead of stoically declining my colleague's offer of help, I should have accepted it.

I arrived at the hospital and was promptly ushered into the Quiet Room. I just knew that this was not good. It was the kind of room I would ask families to wait in when I was a nurse and when things were not going well for their loved one. Now I was being ushered into one. I was then greeted by the manager from the caregiver agency and was told the doctor had just left. When they had made my dad comfortable, we could go in and see him.

Relief—A feeling of reassurance and relaxation following the release of built-up anxiety.

This is what I experienced when I realized that I had arrived in time. I hadn't wasted precious time after all. It was going to be OK.

Mum was bewildered and didn't know what was going on. She relayed the events of the morning with me. Shortly afterward, the doctor returned with news. She was "very sorry and the team had done all that they could, but your father had passed away. Please accept my condolences." Then the doctor turned around and left.

Anger—When someone you love is taken away, it is normal to want to hit and react out of anger.

My anger reared up and was aimed directly at me, at my inability to get there in time. Why had I taken so long?

Disbelief—A part of the shock and numbness; often present in the initial grief phase.

I felt disbelief at what we had just been told as we left the Quiet Room to be taken to the ER to where Dad lay. This can't be happening. I didn't get to say goodbye. It's much too soon.

Guilt—Is an uncomfortable feeling that arises when you think or feel you have done something wrong.

I couldn't help but feel guilty as I stood there holding Dad's hand. I could have gone to see him when Mum told me of his fall earlier that week. If I would have gotten him to the hospital sooner, he might still be alive. It was my fault. I had been so selfish.

Sadness—Is an authentic emotion we feel when something or someone we value is taken from us.

When I listened to Mum's account of her and Dad's last evening and morning together, I felt so sad. How she had held his hand, their heads touching; Mum speaking and Dad laughing and making unintelligible sounds. I could have helped them, but really, should I have been there? I would have robbed them both of those last few hours together, shared in such loving intimacy. No doubt my nursing instincts would have kicked in and an ambulance would have been called. I believed now that I had done the right thing. I could release my guilt—of course, not quite so fast and not quite so easily. I would vacillate on this, too, for many months afterward.

Grief—A deep mental anguish arising from a death.

As thoughts of what I could have said or done came to me, it suddenly hit me—I didn't get to say goodbye to Dad.

Acceptance and letting go—Vital to our healing, they are the signs that we no longer want to carry the heavy load and we decide to set it down. These signs would take more than a year for me to arrive at.

I hope reading my story will help you understand the emotions you are going through or may go through.

WHEN THE STUDENT IS READY, FRIENDS WILL APPEAR

THERE IS A BUDDHIST proverb that says, "When the student is ready, the teacher will appear." I realized that I did not want to stay a moment longer in grief than I needed to. So, I set about reading all that I could about it and researching what one can do to get through it.

I discovered the works of Karla McLaren, Andrea Mathieson, and Malidoma Somé. These three authors helped me further understand grief.

Mathieson's work taught me about how our emotions can get stuck in the body if we hold ourselves tightly together. Through her body work and keening (sounds you make), I was able to break down the dense energy inside of me and free and release it.

Somé's book introduced me to the ancient wisdom of his tribe. He explained that when joy is absent from his village, the villagers know grief has entered and everyone stops what they are doing to assist in releasing the grief from their community. You will learn more about Somé and his ancient wisdom later on.

McLaren's book put me in greater touch with my emotions and helped me to understand them and not be fearful of them.

A good friend had recommended McLaren's book to me. I was so intrigued that I rushed out to purchase it. The book is called The Language of Emotions.

In her book, she describes how in the West, we are uncomfortable seeing others in mourning. We often feel uncomfortable with another's emotions; we feel embarrassed and turn away because we don't want to feel anything that deeply. She believes that the act of turning away from those who are mourning is the real death because, in doing so, we lose out on our compassion, community, feeling, and understanding. Her words struck at the core of my being. How can we do that to another human being or to ourselves?

In the West, most people have not been taught how to "be" with our emotions and certainly not how to "be" with our grief. I am sharing some of McLaren's gems with you to help you to become more familiar with your emotions, for you will need to know them so that you, too, can actively mourn and help yourself heal. Once we have an understanding of something that frightens us, it loses its grip over us.

How many of us can say we enjoy it when fear or anger take over? Hopefully, after reading this, you will learn to be more welcoming of these emotions.

Anger is like a sentry standing on guard to protect your boundaries so you can relate to others more authentically. Anger is asking you what it is you need to protect.

Fear can help you remain focused and intuitive (think of the stories we have all heard about a mother finding the strength to lift a car off her child). Fear hones your senses, alerts your survival skills, and increases your ability to respond to changing environments. Its gifts are an ability to feel focused, centered, capable, and agile.

Guilt and **shame** surface to alert you when your internal boundary has been broken by something you have or have not done.

Guilt arises to help you learn right from wrong. When you understand why you feel guilty, you are able to use that awareness to determine what the right thing to do is. That allows you to feel proud because you did the right thing. This, in turn, brings you happiness and and a sense of ease.

Sadness shows up to slow you down so that you can feel your loss. It also helps you release what is no longer serving you. It assists in softening you, especially, if you hold everything in or are continually pushing yourself forward. Sadness helps us with our tears and, when we cry, the tears help relax our bodies and remove its toxins.

Depression is not just one emotion but a whole collection of emotions, postures, decisions, and health issues. McLaren calls depression "a brilliant stop-sign for the soul." It takes you out of commission, so to speak. You experience depression from conflicts in your outer and inner worlds. Depression's task is to restrict your energy, which also protects you by slowing down your ability to walk down the wrong path, or do the wrong things for the wrong reasons.

Grief comes forward to assist you in moving through your losses in life by dropping you down into the river to be cleansed and renewed. Let it carry you along; don't fight the current and waste your precious energies.

I found, when reading about each emotion, it started to make more sense to me and helped me understand what I was doing by constantly ignoring my feelings in grief, as well as out of grief. I was now tapping into the wisdom of others.

I also realized it is our childhood conditioning that helps us control our emotions the way we do. Our adult caregivers are often not comfortable with us doing what is normal and natural as small children. We don't have the language to express our emotions, so we cry, whine, or get angry and have a tantrum. The adults around us don't always appreciate these acts and often do not take the time to investigate what it is we want to express. It is then that our emotions begin to go unnoticed and retreat underground. For most of us, we are never given permission to allow ourselves to cry freely. It's not uncommon to hear a parent say to a crying child, "If you don't stop, I'll give you something to cry about," or "Do you want a smack? Then you will have something to cry about." I realized that we have to give ourselves permission to cry because no one else is likely to do it for us. We have to make a conscious effort to undo the years of conditioning that taught us not to express our sadness. I could easily distract myself to get myself to stop crying after only a short time. I realized that I needed to let the tears flow if I wanted to completely release my grief.

While etiquette dictates that it is not courteous or polite to those around us to display our emotions, it is necessary. Some of you may be able to easily let go and allow your emotions to come out; others may be less willing. However, to be able to grieve and mourn fully, we need to have permission, and it has to come from ourselves. We need to give ourselves permission to cry, scream, be angry, be confused, be in denial ... whatever it is that we are experiencing at the moment. Whatever it is, it is quite real; and know that you are not losing your grip on reality, going crazy, being irrational, or anything else. If you find yourself expressing such negative self-talk, it's important to stop it. Take a deep breath and say to yourself, "I give you permission to cry."

THE FOREST OF GRIEF

GRIEF, LIKE DEATH, is never welcome, it is inconvenient, and you cannot prepare for it. Many of us use the terms grief, mourning, and bereavement almost interchangeably. We have no concrete understanding of what these mean and how they are distinguished from each other. Grief is what is experienced internally; mourning is an external affair; bereavement is who we are after a death.

It is here that you will either accept grief as part of the journey or you will turn and flee from it. You are likely aware of the initial feelings that will arise upon hearing the news that your loved one has died. It's not hard to imagine the pain and heartache associated with death. Maybe you have already experienced planning a funeral and the endless arrangements that go into one. If so, one hopes you were supported by family, friends, and your community. If this is the case, you then likely have slipped into mourning despite trying with all your might to contain your emotions. If you are to heal, it is important to go through the mourning process, according to Dr. Alan D. Wolfelt, who wrote Healing the Adult Child's Grieving Heart: 100 Practical Ideas After Your Parent Dies.

You may also have entered into a period of bereavement. Unfortunately, in Western culture, there is no ceremony marking the time when a person enters this period... other than a funeral. Long ago, it was customary to wear black for a specific period, so as to alert others of a death in the family. Some still cling to this tradition, but it's usually followed just for the day of the funeral. Once the funeral is over, people tend to return to their normal attire.

Grief's Abyss

It is here that we find ourselves in the forest of grief, for we are inwardly grieving but trying hard not to openly mourn. Thus, the bereaved person walks between two worlds. It's no wonder they are in pain. Like a wounded animal crawls further into its den in the forest to keep itself safe, so, too, does the bereaved person, for life has suddenly become bewildering and unreal.

Not all will enter the forest to heal. There are those who prefer to shun grief and mourning by actively being in denial, or by moving on quickly and telling all who ask, "I'm fine." Some enter the forest naturally and may find they are in distress and agitation when they think of the deceased—a constant reminder that the person is no longer there. In the state of agitation they move from activity to activity, trying to stay busy, preoccupied, engaged. Their bodies are moving, but their minds are somewhere else.

Once deep in the forest, lost and alone, bereft of comfort, safety, companionship, a mentor, a friend, or whatever role the deceased acted as in your life, there is now time to reflect upon your relationship and all that you have lost. According to doctor and author Robert A. Neimeyer, PhD, in his book Bereavement and the Quest for Meaning, to have it all make sense we need to rewrite stories of our loss and grief. This reconstruction process can help heal us of our grief. Our lives are like books and each person we interact with, particularly our family members and close friends, play a role and lends meaning to our existence. Thus, when someone in your life dies, it is as if the pages of your life are being torn out, leaving a gaping hole. Those now missing pages gave your life meaning and helped you understand your life. The pages before the death and after don't match, and the whole context is gone. No wonder your life seems filled with chaos suddenly. A new chapter has yet to be written. Until you have that next chapter, your world will continue to cling to the past and you will have difficulty remaining in the present. There isn't the energy to be present in your immediate life if you are still stuck in the past. The only way to change this is to view it as an opportunity to reorganize your life and to be the author of your life's new chapter.

I will continue to hold the candle and point the compass to show you how to find your way to your new chapter. Read on.

REFLECTIONS

1. Can you identify your emotions as they arise?

If so, where in the body do you feel them? Where do they make their presence felt?

2. Can you recall what you were told as a child to keep you from expressing sad or angry emotions?

By recalling these words, you will be able to identify hidden beliefs you have about your emotions. Once you unearth those hidden beliefs, you will be able to let go of them and adopt new, healthier ones.

3. From your list of identified emotions, see if you can now identify what your emotions are telling you.

For example, your anger may arise to protect you from other unpleasant feelings, such as pain, guilt, frustration, fear, or dependency.

Fear asks you what action is needed; it is often mistaken as anxiety or worry.

CHAPTER 3

> Owning our story can be hard but not nearly as difficult as spending our lives running from it. Embracing our vulnerabilities is risky but not nearly as dangerous as giving up on love and belonging and joy—the experiences that make us the most vulnerable. Only when we are brave enough to explore the darkness will we discover the infinite power of our light.
>
> Brené Brown

CANDLE IN THE DARKNESS

ONCE I WENT ON a white-water rafting trip with my family. Before we got into the boat, an instructor explained what we needed to do in order to stay safe during the trip down the rapids. One thing I'll never forget was being told that if we did fall into the water, we should not attempt to swim. The currents, he said, would keep us in place or take us down to a spot where we would not be able to escape by swimming. He told us to curl up into a ball instead. If we did this, then we would be popped back up to the surface.

In the months after my dad's death, I sat in my dark abyss of grief. Feeling as if I had nothing to lose, I allowed myself to get into that tight ball position (the fetal position) and let my emotions flow, hoping that, after some time, I would pop back up into life so that I could continue my journey downstream. I told myself that whenever I did encounter the rapids, I would do the same thing—allow the rapids to do their thing and let myself go without fighting them.

Another thing my rafting experience taught me was that I needed a guide. I would never have survived that trip without the instructors and guides. They knew the route and the terrain. Why would I expect to find my way out of grief all by myself? I had never been there before. Clearly, I needed a guide to help me through the journey. I decided to see a psychologist who then told me grief was a personal experience and everyone experiences it differently. At the time, I did not have the language to describe what I was feeling or even know what to ask. I didn't know what I didn't know.

What I really wanted from the psychologist was a timeline or a map of what to expect. I hoped he could give this to me because I didn't want to stay in my grief any longer than I needed to. He did not have such a timeline, so I decided not to go back to see him. But that didn't stop me from realizing I still needed to have company on this journey. I just needed to find the right person. This person would eventually show up when the time was right.

Until that person arrived, I told myself that I would keep trying to find my own understanding by continuing to research the grieving process. It is these findings that I am sharing with you throughout this book. I culled only those that made sense to me, gave me hope, and helped me to progress. I hope sharing these with you will bring you the same comfort and understanding they brought to me.

Why do we fear loss? It seems life is preparing us for it as we transition from childhood into adulthood and then into our elder years. Do we experience these smaller losses as a way to prepare us for the bigger ones, such as our own death? It seems as though we have become death-averse and will do anything to avoid it because we know it is painful. Instead of dealing with each loss, we allow them to accumulate and some parts get buried deep within us. When a parent or another loved one dies, a break occurs. Often the grief we feel is not just for this loss—albeit among the greatest loss of life—it is also for other losses we have experienced, but not yet dealt with.

The very first loss to be experienced as a child probably occurs when your parent takes away your soother or pacifier. Later, it might be a favourite toy that is lost. Or what about the panic a child feels when shopping with a parent and suddenly loses sight of him or her and are faced with feeling alone for the first time? Any of these losses tend to provoke crying from most children, and it is through these lessons and the guidance of loved ones that you learn how to deal with loss little by little. The death of a family pet, a friend moving away, parents divorcing, a first breakup—these are other losses than can cause varying degrees of grief. However, a pet can be replaced, or so you are told, and you can always make new friends. Parents— well, that is definitely for another book—but divorcing parents are not always available to help their children with their feelings of loss.

When you break up with a first boyfriend or girlfriend, you may be reminded by well-meaning parents that "there are more fish in the sea." But your sadness and grief are very real and should not be downplayed. Parents have a tendency not to offer the same empathy or compassion in these situations than they would with a death. A better approach would be for parents to use these losses as a chance to evaluate how acceptable a child's emotions and feelings are, to see how the child responds to the events. Sadly, children are often ridiculed or shamed for crying, and it doesn't take long before they recognize society isn't comfortable with public displays of emotion.

Getting terminated from a job, suffering from health issues, losing a sense of who you are—these are other losses that you will possibly experience at some point in your life. These losses, too, can keep you drowning in grief or turn into depression if not recognized and confronted. To feel any loss means we have formed an attachment to a person or object. It is the price we pay for giving our hearts and loving another being.

TYPES OF GRIEF

DURING THE MONTHS that I was in mourning, the most troubling aspect of it for me was the sense of disorganization that I felt of finding myself unable to cope with much of anything. This confused state had me believing that I was going crazy. The sadness and depression were things I had anticipated and expected; however, the confusion and inability to think clearly were not. I finally received relief when I described what was going on to my boss, a physician. He responded in a very matter-of-fact manner, stating, "Oh, it sounds like you have a reactionary depression." I breathed a sigh a relief. Discovering that what I was experiencing had a name, somehow, made it all feel normal and OK.

Reactionary depression is, as its name implies, a part of the depression family. But unlike pure depression, reactionary depression is not usually treated clinically, as it normally resolves itself over time. If, however, you suffer from such a depression for six months or longer, you should seek help from a medical professional who can diagnose you with certainty and treat you accordingly. I did not seek help because these symptoms only lasted a few months. I think for me, having a name to put to what I was experiencing helped me. It let me know that I was not alone.

There are also a number of different types of grief. I have outlined these to help you understand them. A word of caution though; although I have given an explanation of my understanding of the various forms of grief, this doesn't make me a medical expert in them. If you are experiencing any physical or emotional symptoms that are of concern to you, please seek professional help. Do not rely on what I am sharing with you. I do so only to give a name to the many types of grief and to shed some light on what they look and feel like. This is not meant as a clinical diagnosis.

ANTICIPATORY GRIEF

THIS IS THE GRIEF that a person may go through when someone they love is expected to die. Anticipatory grief helps us prepare emotionally for what is to come. When you are taking care of someone who is ill and death is imminent, you find yourself making peace with the situation and, eventually, accepting what will come. Anticipatory grief involves the same emotions except that there may not be the same intenseness that is felt when a death is unexpected. When you are experiencing anticipatory grief, you have time to work through your feelings. The grief process may have started at the time of diagnosis and the person only feels relief from it when the person who is dying passes away because they know that that person is no longer in pain and suffering.

A friend of mine shared that she felt tremendous sadness, but also tremendous relief, when her father died. She and her siblings had taken turns looking after their father for many months. They all worked full-time, but each took turns spending the night at his home, caring for him. This routine continued into the weekend. All of the siblings were extremely tired and emotionally drained when their father passed away. My friend reported it was a mixed blessing, and they were happy with the thought their father was no longer in distress. She explained that watching him suffer was the hardest part of the entire ordeal. Yes, my friend was grieving and mourning, but knowing that she and her siblings had done all they could to help their dad, comforted them. They were able to grant their dad's wish to remain in his home. After their father passed away, it was time to take care of themselves and regain their individual stamina. They also had to process the grief that had begun when they were told their father would not recover. But there was no guilt or reproach. Each sibling had been able to spend time with their father and had been able to say goodbye.

Others who are experiencing anticipatory grief may manage to go through the grieving process while their loved one is still alive. They are saddened when the death occurs, of course, but they can resume their lives fairly quickly afterward because they have already grieved the loss. For those watching from the sidelines, it may appear as if these individuals didn't care for their loved one. This is an unfair assessment; however, as they have already been through the stages of grief by the time the person dies. It is so important that we do not judge others by how they react to the death of a loved one. Each of us will deal with grief in our own way and not all will experience anticipatory grief.

NORMAL GRIEF

NORMAL GRIEF is what is experienced when someone suffers the loss of a loved one. It describes how the bereaved person copes with the loss. Usually the bereaved person will move through their grief and come to acceptance. Although it may be difficult, they are able to continue with their daily lives. They may feel the intense emotions that occur right after a death, and these are heightened when a death has not been expected or anticipated. They may also experience anxiety and anger or feelings of distress. There will also likely be periods of sadness, insomnia, loss of appetite, and extreme fatigue.

The good news is that for most, these symptoms will eventually become less severe. Although there is no timeline for grief, the majority of people suffering from "normal" grief can expect their symptoms to lessen in anywhere from six months to two years.

Once my grief was named, I was able to move more quickly through it. After three months, the intensity of my feelings began to lessen. I did, however, continue to experience what the experts call *grief bursts*. A word, a photo, a thought—all can provoke a short burst of intense grief. It took me about a year before I was ready to accept the new reality and say goodbye in earnest. I made a conscious decision to piece my life together again. I could finally speak about my dad without becoming emotional, as had been the case up until then. By year two, I was making major decisions that certainly impacted my life. I chose to take early retirement, for instance.

COMPLICATED GRIEF

COMPLICATED GRIEF may occur when normal grief gets stuck, or it can arise as a result of the closeness of the relationship (partner, child, or parent), or because of the nature of the death. For example, a death which results from a tragic accident can make for a longer, more complicated grieving process.

The symptoms of complicated grief are often the same as those of normal grief, such as anger, sadness, guilt, despair, a sense of being overwhelmed, denial, betrayal, or emptiness. You might feel the death was your fault, that it's unfair this happened to you and your loved one, or that you cannot get over the event, and more. You may find yourself withdrawing from friends and family and isolating yourself. For some, the grief is so overwhelming that it may trigger addiction issues or other reckless behavior. Physical symptoms, including insomnia, extreme fatigue, pain, anxiety, and loss of appetite and motivation, will endure for more than six months.

There are also some indications from the research that certain factors such as religious beliefs, age and gender may influence how we cope with the loss of a loved one. The common theme is in the amount of support a person has. Your faith will lend support and comfort, especially, if you are involved in your church community. Younger people who are bereaved tend to have a larger network of friends and family than an older person. Males seem to have fewer social networks and, thus, may not get the same amount of support that a female would. Men may also be less likely than women to seek help, making them more prone to complicated grief.

DISENFRANCHISED GRIEF (KENNETH J. DOKA, PH.D)

ALL LOSSES—great and small—have meaning for the person experiencing them. Unfortunately, society does not recognize many of these losses. It barely acknowledges death.

Very often, when a parent dies, the first thing you may be asked is how old was your mother or father. People seem to think if someone is older the loss is not as great or not as worthy of grieving. Regardless of how old a person is it is still a big loss for those who loved him or her.

The same is true for women who miscarry or for parents whose child is diagnosed with a mental disability. Loss is loss. It isn't lessened if the person committed suicide or died from an overdose or Aids.

These are the secondary losses that no one thinks of: the hopes, dreams, and aspirations you may have had, or the shame attached to the death so that you are fearful speaking about it and sharing your feelings because you don't want to be judged or have your loved one judged. These are the "griefs" that go unnoticed or unacknowledged. And these are the bereaved that may have to endure the loss alone unless someone steps up.

The most important thing for all of us to be mindful of is that no one's loss is greater or lesser than another person's. When someone or something we love is lost to us, we will feel pain and we will, if we are emotionally healthy, grieve. Someone who has lost a pet can feel the same degree of despair and sadness as someone who has lost a child. We shouldn't judge anyone in the way they grieve or handle their grief. They feel and do what they need to do because they have loved.

YOUR COPING STYLE

HOW YOU HAVE dealt with loss previously can help shed light on how you will deal with the death of a loved one. Do you cope well? Do you mourn and then move on? Or do you have a tendency to run from your pain and not acknowledge it? How you responded likely describes your coping style. Our personalities come into play and determine how we handle certain events. If you have ever taken a personality test, such as the Myers-Briggs Assessment, you may know more about how you will cope with major life losses. As you can see, grief is complex and how someone copes with it depends on many factors.

Some people are quite comfortable with their emotions and have no trouble displaying them. Such people may find themselves getting emotional over a television commercial. For these people, their emotions lie just below the surface and are easily accessed. For logical thinkers or more analytical types, it may be harder to access their emotions and understand them. These are the folks who prefer to research and find out about their grief; these individuals prefer concrete theories and linear models to help them cope. There are also creative individuals. For them, grief can either block their creativity, resulting in a stagnant period, or force their creativity to the surface and result in an incredibly productive period.

My coping style is to turn tail and run and not look back! I can share with you that going through a divorce caused me to leave my job, my family, and my country of origin. No wonder I didn't deal well with the death of my dad. There was no place that I could run to. I had many more commitments at this point in my life and running away was simply not an option; I had to work through my grief. According to the Myers-Briggs Asssessment, I am an analytical person. So, it stands to reason that I would want a map and guidelines to navigate through the grieving process. And it explains why I relate so well to Dr. Kübler-Ross's model of the five stages of grief. I have identified with most of those wise, theoretical medical professionals and their stages or theories as they, too, have researched and written them to help us understand.

Take the time now to do an inventory of all the losses you have experienced in your life and describe how you coped with each one. It may be very revealing and helpful to reflect on your past record of loss and coping. Then, with further guidance on how to actively mourn and work through your grief, you may be much more able to take action and move through your grief in a healthier, healing way.

It is helpful to review your past as well as the past of the parent or loved one who has died. This grieving process is a way to actively make peace with previous losses that may still be keeping you trapped and may even reveal losses that you were totally unaware of. Often, past losses build up so that when we do finally experience grief through the death of a loved one, there is an accumulative effect. This may be why you feel you are much more in grief than you thought was possible.

REFLECTIONS

1 **What has been your loss experience?**

Write each one down and describe how well you coped after each one.

2 **Did you tend to run from loss? Do you downplay loss? Or do you accept loss easily and just move on?**

Whatever your answer is, ask why you chose to react in that way and what had been your motivation for doing so.

3 **Have you identified the type of grief you experienced?**

Did it surprise you? Are you less anxious because there is a name for that type of grief? What is your plan of action now?

CHAPTER 4

> Until you value yourself, you won't value
> your time. Until you value your time,
> you will not do anything with it.
>
> M. Scott Peck

LIVING IN TWO WORLDS

AS MENTIONED previously in the Forest of Grief, people grieving have their feet in two worlds. They are with the deceased person in one world and are also re-entering their everyday world. No wonder the bereaved are exhausted and distressed; it is hard to be in two separate worlds. When you are emotionally overwrought, it is hard to focus or plan even the simplest of tasks. It takes so much more energy to remain focused, leaving you drained at the end of the day. Many bereaved people returning to the workforce often have trouble getting through the day. Depending on the amount of bereavement leave you have (most people get between three to five days off) you likely have not had enough time to process your grief. Often, once the funeral is over, those who have remained strong and stoic through it all tend to unravel once there is nothing to distract them from their feelings.

For others, returning to work can be cathartic. It may be something of a sanctuary of normalcy and stability, a place where nothing has changed and where they can continue playing their regular role. It's life at home that has changed. We love our titles and when one is taken away, we cease to feel we exist. We may no longer be a wife, husband, daughter, son, mother, father, or sibling. When someone loses their job, it is not only the financial and social aspects that are lost, but it is also that person's status in the world. How many of us are tied to our professional work titles and our careers? They define us and tell the world who we are to a great extent. When asked, "What do you do?" we usually reply by telling them our profession. Who are we without our labels and titles? It's yet another loss that comes with the death.

Some may find their grief is too great for them to function at work and will need to take time off in order to work through their grief. Unfortunately, many employers are not well-equipped to deal with bereaved employees. At many companies, once a person is back in the office, they are expected to work as normal. How many of us have a workplace culture of "your home life and work life are separate and whatever is going on in your private life is not their business or problem?" Even our colleagues may get annoyed with us if we continue to sob at our desks or want to continue to share our story for a long time. We may see people walking the other way because they don't want to have to speak to us. Ouch.

We need to cultivate a more compassionate society and a more compassionate workplace in order to help ourselves and others heal from grief. By creating a culture of compassion in the workforce, we could actually cut down on absenteeism and could likely increase productivity as well. We are reaching that critical point in Western culture where the baby boomers are retiring and are now looking after their elderly parents—although some may still be working due to a divorce or the downturn in the economy. No longer was "Freedom 55" a popular insurance commercial in Canada that once lured us into thinking of early retirement. There will be some 90 million baby boomers in the next 20 years that will be facing the loss of one or both of their parents, spouses, or both. This does not take into account those affected by other losses.

It may be time to face the costs of ignoring grief in our society. We have been denying it at great cost to the human psyche and to the impact of loss of productivity in the workforce. Failing to deal with grief leads to depression, and the downward spiral continues, adversely affecting our relationships, families, and careers.

How will this so-called *sandwich generation* cope with their losses and the added responsibility of caring for elderly parents and grief? Are four days of compassionate leave long enough to arrange a funeral, get the deceased's estate in order, deal with one's own grief and come back as a productive member in the workplace? It is doubtful. Many workplaces do have employee assistance programs, but how many employees recognize their need for help?

Companies do need to recognize that gone are the days when private life and work life were separate. Today people spend more time at work than with their families. When a death occurs, many employees go to work regardless of how they are feeling, but their productivity is greatly reduced. They often worry that they may lose their job because of it. "When your heart is broken, your head doesn't work right," says Russell Friedman, the co-director for The Grief Recovery Institute.

COPING WITH LOSS AT HOME OR IN THE WORKPLACE

HOME LIFE is a little easier to handle than our working one. It is our decision if we continue with our usual cleaning, cooking, and shopping routines. It will not hurt anyone if things do get left undone and unattended for a certain period of time. Possibly, there are family members or even friends that will help out. After my father passed away, I wasn't hungry, so it was a huge chore for me to meal plan, grocery shop, and cook. When you are in mourning, it is hard to focus on keeping the home tidy and clean. These chores don't seem important in the scheme of things. It's hard just getting yourself to shower and bathe. It may help you to know that all this is normal and no one will care if things fall apart for a spell. Financial issues may be a little harder to ignore as bills won't pay themselves. This can be particularly difficult if you are a widow and your husband always did these tasks for you. Even though they are relatively simple tasks, when you are in mourning, even the most basic chore can seem insurmountable. Our brains don't seem capable to take on new chores and new information at this time. Asking a family member for help may be the best route to take. Then, when you are feeling more like yourself and your mind clears, you can ask for a lesson and learn how to do that task yourself. Too often, when someone is in mourning, family members or friends will just take over and you will ultimately find yourself relying on them rather than learning how to do these things for yourself. If you can, it is a good idea to remain active when you're in mourning. Keeping to a routine can help as well, just maybe a simpler routine than that you are used to.

Each morning when you get up, you could take some time to think about the things that need to be done and see when and how you would like to fit them in. Don't get upset or angry with yourself if you decide to do nothing. It is important to listen to what you need in those early days of grieving. It may serve you better to be taking care of your emotional needs than to be out picking up the dry cleaning, for example. The best thing to do for yourself is invest in your own care and healing journey. Also try to make plans for the future and ensure you include some downtime and some fun times for yourself.

Those returning to work after a death may find it helpful to speak to their immediate manager and ask them to inform the staff. In this way, you don't have to revisit your sadness with all your colleagues and work friends individually. You may also want to discuss and plan your return to work. Find out how many vacation days or how much holiday time you have accrued, or negotiate some flex time. And once back at work, you may want to prioritize your tasks and concentrate on getting the most critical tasks done first.

It was Dr. David Hawkins's book, *Power Versus Force*, which helped me to understand why it is so difficult to organize and make decisions on the job while in grief. From Hawkins's work on applied kinesiology and scientific research, he was able to find a practical way of calibrating energy fields of emotions by assigning a logarithmic equation to each feeling and then comparing them. Hawkins found that grief calibrates at 75, which indicates that the energy of grief is rather low on his scale. If a person in grief gets angry, his or her energy increases and calibrates higher at 150, which is an improvement over grief. However, a grieving person is able to function and make effective decisions in daily life and at the workplace when his or her energy field is calibrating at 400. No wonder so many people struggle when they return to work after a death.

Acknowledge the loss; don't be afraid to mention the person's name. However, please don't compare your losses with others; be supportive with anyone who has suffered a loss. It is about them, not you, in those moments. Each loss is felt differently; some losses are felt more deeply than others. It is as unique as the person you have lost. Death and grief are conceptual concepts until they happen to you. You know they are out there, but how many of us can relate to what is in front of us until it happens and you experience it for yourself? It is not like training for a marathon, where you can read about it or practise it, because it only becomes real when we experience it for ourselves. It is only then that you can understand the pain and begin to have compassion for others who have experienced it. Grief cracks open our hearts, rendering us vulnerable. We are social creatures and, as humans, we need connection and touch. When someone we love dies, the connection is lost and time is required to get over that loss. However, reaching out for support helps us to connect with others. Allow grief to express itself and let it do so in its own time. The phrase, "I know how you feel," is hollow until you have actually walked in that person's shoes. It is almost better to refrain from saying anything, if that is all you have to say, and you haven't actually experienced the loss of a loved one. If you are the bereaved, it is OK to say to others: "I realize you are uncomfortable, but you mean well. Thank you for caring and taking the time to be with me. This is much better than being avoided or ignored because someone feels uncomfortable being with me or acknowledging my loss."

It is always best not to minimize or compare loss, as each loss brings its own heartache and pain, and each person experiences grief differently. It is also a good idea not to tell someone how to grieve. Grief takes us into the past, the present, and the future. The present is all we have and it hurts. Our past is fraught with memories and landmines to be stepped on and reviewed. Slipping into the future will, one hopes, bring peace. But sadly, the future will inevitably, bring more loss. Patience and understanding that the grief process can take time and that the person who is grieving cannot snap out of it—for if they could, I am sure they would—will go a long way to help expectations to be met.

THE IMPORTANCE OF SELF CARE

GRIEF IS a journey with twists and turns along the way. Be gentle with yourself. You certainly would take care of yourself if you had a broken leg. The only difference is that we can't put a cast on our hearts as a reminder that it, too, needs some time to heal. Other people will also forget that we are healing because we won't have any visible reminders, such as a cast, to alert them to our pain and disability. Sometimes I think it would be easier if we went back to the tradition of wearing black to signify that we are in mourning. Such visible reminders tell the world to treat us with care and to be gentle with us in this time of loss. Don't expect too much from us just now, as we are only partially available to ourselves and to the world. This is an opportunity to allow yourself to withdraw from the world to take care of yourself, especially, if you have other outside responsibilities. If you are unable to make decisions, it makes sense to contact and connect with others. If, for example, you are a volunteer coach, reach out and let the other volunteers know what is going on. Ask to be removed from volunteer duties. Don't beat yourself up. Instead take this time to focus on you and know that this is OK.

You know the importance of taking care of yourself, but so few of us do it. I am the same way. It is so easy when a deadline approaches to talk yourself out of exercising or to take time out to nourish yourself with a healthy meal. Too often, you may choose to unmindfully grab a convenient snack and eat at your desk. A bigger mistake, and one that I have done, is to get up even earlier than normal and go into work in an attempt to catch up. It may feel like you are, but it can also lead to further fatigue and even more mistakes. Another caution is to unplug and leave all your techie devices in another room to charge overnight. The LED lights in these devices can actually create imbalances in the brain's chemistry. There are two important chemicals that which come into play. Serotonin is the "on switch" that helps you to stay alert and awake, and melatonin is the "off switch" that helps you to relax and tells the body to shut down for sleep. The brain needs darkness to make melatonin from the serotonin, and this melatonin breaks down under light. I hope this explanation helps you to understand the importance of leaving these devices outside of your sleeping area. Also cover the alarm clock, as these newer models all have LED lights in them. Being bereaved, sleep is so important and many thoughts and worries can already highjack your sleep; don't add any others to the list right now. In addition, choose a time to go to bed and stick to it every night. In turn, rise every morning at the same time. If you can, keep to a routine, such as your gym time or schedule walks at lunchtime. Do this for a week and note how much better you feel.

These are definitely hard to do when you feel sad and are in active mourning. It's important keep your body moving. Take up yoga if going to the gym leaves you feeling uninspired. Or simply walk for 15 minutes a day outside. The fresh air, sunshine, and being outdoors can help you gain a healthy perspective. And don't forget to hydrate. Drinking six to eight glasses of water is essential for our bodies and brains, especially in the initial stages of mourning when you are losing fluids through your tears.

It is important also to set aside time to cry. Tears not only remove toxins, they also help our hearts to heal.

Like everything else, drinking water, especially eight glasses a day, is necessary to keep you well-hydrated. Plan your day and when you will have each of your eight glasses. Coffee, tea, and alcohol don't count ... sorry. It must be 100 percent, pure H2O. If you find yourself drinking more coffee and alcohol as a way to cope with loss, it is even more important to get your six to eight glasses of water, because coffee and alcohol act as diuretics. This means you will be going to the washroom more often, as coffee and alcohol draw greater amounts of fluid out of your body. If you are feeling thirsty, this is a sign that you are dehydrated. Thus, never wait until you are thirsty to drink water.

You may find that if you are the executor for the deceased's estate, your workload is greatly increased. You may also be juggling work responsibilities as well as your home. With all the added responsibilities, it is more important than ever to get adequate rest. Make time for yourself. Delegate duties when you can and ask for help from family members as well as coworkers. Because your energy and decision-making processes are often impaired after a death, you may find you are expending more energy than normal. Taking time off from work, if you have vacation leave or sick time available, is an act of self care; particularly, if the person who has died had been sick for a long time. You may not be aware of it, but you were under stress during the entire period of their illness.

People often overlook the need for touch, especially, if the deceased was a husband or wife. A massage can offer relaxation as well as the touch that you have been missing. One word of caution though; as wonderful as massages can be, they can bring emotions to the surface and you may find yourself sobbing. This is normal and your massage therapist, if well trained, should be aware of the effects that massage can have on a person. Don't feel embarrassed or decide not to have one "just in case." It's better to have the massage and risk the tears.

If you don't like massages or you cannot afford one, you can always give or ask for hugs. The main thing is to be sure you have human contact and connection. These are vital during the grieving process.

Human beings thrive on touch and such contact is even more critical during times of massive change. Touch can actually help us heal, bring us comfort, and allow cathartic tears to flow. You will feel much better inside and out.

This is also a great time to take up meditation. Not a meditator or can't stand the idea of sitting still for 20 minutes? You can still sit quietly in a chair for a few moments and enjoy the tranquillity. If you listen intently, you may hear a clock tick, the birds singing in the garden, or the house just creaking. Drink it all in. You and your brain need time to rest and recharge. This is also a great time for a cup of tea.

It is normal for you to not feel like reading or even watching TV when you are agitated or restless. This is all part of the mourning process. Just ensure you take some time to quietly relax. Five-minute naps are also a great way to rejuvenate and you should not feel guilty taking them. You will feel more energetic after you have allowed yourself to rest. Even listening to your favourite music can help slow your mind down and help you to relax and stop thinking.

Perhaps you have heard similar advice in the past and are tempted to skip over this chapter. I hope you don't because even though you may know about relaxation techniques, it is important to be reminded from time to time to tap into them. Any one of these activities can help you move through your grief with greater ease. When your body is well-rested, well-nourished, and well-hydrated, you are in a much better position to deal with the additional tasks that need to be handled when a loved one passes away.

Volunteering at a later date (after the early stages of your mourning) can also be beneficial to your spirit and soul because, when you give, you also receive. This is a great way to step outside your grief for short periods, and have company and something and someone else to focus on. Don't under estimate the power of giving to another during your healing journey.

Taking action every day, even if it's just doing some small task, is critical. It's like the old adage says: A body in motion stays in motion!

Learning about grief and how you can move through it is also helpful because the more you understand about this process, the better equipped you will be to help yourself and others.

Reaching out to others and asking how they coped with a death can be immensely comforting. Obviously, you do not need to do everything others recommend or that they found helpful; just do the things that resonate with you.

Self-help groups can be another source of support and help in the initial stages; but I caution you to be careful that you don't get caught in the victim role. There are some groups that can inadvertently help people remain stuck in their grief and fail to move on from it. Some of these groups are alluring because you may find friends in them and feel a sense of belonging when you are with them. Some people cling to their grief because it gives them a sense of identity. If they were to admit they are no longer mourning, then they cannot remain in the group.

REFLECTIONS

1 **Plan your return to work; make a list of the people you need to contact and speak to.**

By contemplating how you may feel upon returning to work, you will likely come up with ideas that can make the transition back easier. For example, you may want to speak to your manager and let him or her know what has happened and how you are feeling about it.

2 **Choose a trusted colleague and let him or her know that you may need support from time to time as you navigate back into the working world and continue working through your grief.**

Sometimes, it is the simplest of things that can set you off emotionally. If you know you have someone you can speak to, someone who will listen to you, it can be incredibly reassuring. You definitely will need support both in the workplace and at home during this trying time.

3 **Make a list of important events that are coming up, as well as any household tasks which need immediate attention. Prioritize them. (I recognize it is hard to think about making lists, but just add one thing each day as part of your daily action steps and it will soon build.**

Determine how important the event is and cancel it if it's not something critical. Don't be afraid to ask friends to assist you with household tasks that need to be addressed. Good friends will want to help you in your time of need and you can reciprocate later when the tables are turned.

4 **Write down three to four activities that you enjoy and help you relax.**

Make a plan to work at least two of these things into your life on a daily basis. Grief sometimes profits from distractions. Even soaking in a tub for 15 minutes or having a good cry can help.

CHAPTER 5

At the time of death all clocks in the household would be stopped and the curtains drawn, black clothes would be immediately worn, mirrors covered. If no suitable black cloth was available, other garments would be died black. So begins the mourning period in Victorian times ...

Angelpig.com

MAKING SENSE OF LOSS

HOW MANY TIMES have we heard that time heals all wounds? Unfortunately, you could wait a long time if you believe this myth. It takes action to recover from the death of a loved one. The action is believing you can heal from the loss and doing what you can to take steps toward that healing. Relief from your pain can only begin when you stop looking outside of yourself and settle down to do your inner work. It is in making sense of your loss, in terms of the relationship and what it meant to you, and all that you have lost. It is in the choosing of your thoughts to what you want them to be—and not what you think they "should be"—is when you will start to shift your perceptions. My immediate thoughts could have been that my life is over or that I have to give up my wants and needs to now take care of my mum. Instead, I thought to myself, "Mum is still quite independent and I can visit her weekly and call her as needed. I can continue to be independent and not have her needs take over my life. My life is not over. I can choose to seek help and continue striving to balance my needs with my mum's."

It is so sad that we wait until a crisis occurs before we seek advice on how to deal with it. No one willingly picks up a book about death to find out what they should do before it happens or what emotions and feelings they can expect to experience when someone they love dies. We instinctively know that when someone dies, it is going to hurt and there will be great pain. So, instead of educating ourselves beforehand so we can better handle it when it occurs, we prefer to avoid thinking and learning about it. Instead of dealing with each loss at the time, parts get buried deep within us, like a heavy weight to be dragged around with us. The weight gets heavier with each successive loss. This continues until you cannot carry any more weight. You have to release it when it becomes too much of a burden to bear. It often happens that we will break, in a sense, when it is the least convenient for us to do so. This rupture often comes with the death of a loved one, such as a parent.

The heart so stalwart has carried these losses for so many years that it has finally said, "No more. I must confront my grief now."

Stephen Levine, in his book *A Year to Live* asks, "If you had one year to live, what would you do?" Wouldn't you prepare for your death by living every second, truly living life, exploring everything? In his one-year-to-live experiment, Levine found that living as if you only had one year left was not some morbid undertaking, but is, surprisingly, quite the reverse. Such thinking does not invite death, but rather encourages the completion of long-avoided tasks. For some reason, when you know you are going to die, you let go of your fear.

Imagine that you had to undergo tests for a possible life-threatening disease. How would you deal with waiting two weeks for the results? Chances are you would spend your precious two weeks fretting about the results. Instead, what if you spent those two weeks planning everything that you want to do on the off-chance the results are not favourable or, perhaps, even start implementing those changes?

Levine found that most would choose to leave their place of work. Why? Perhaps, it would be to experience the freedom of doing exactly what they wanted to finally, or having the chance to travel. What would be on your list of things to do or see before you die? This is your chance to look at your life and choose what you want your life to stand for, what places you would like to visit, and what experiences you would want to have. Think about this. You may just discover something important or surprising about yourself and your life.

Death isn't convenient. We never know when it will occur and are never ready when it comes our way. Do you want a closetful of regrets or could-haves and should-haves? Or will you use Levine's question to put fuel back into your perfectly controlled life—a life you are living, but living without any real passion, with just a vague sense of longing for the life you had hoped to have, at some undefined point in the future? We tend to delay and put off so much in our lives. Look at this question not as something to dread, but rather as something to boldly confront. Use it in a dinner conversation maybe. What do you have to lose? Not asking it may prevent you from living your life to its fullest. Death has this effect on us whether it's someone else's death or thoughts of our own. I couldn't make sense of my family's loss until I had put the pieces together like a jigsaw puzzle. This book talks about death and dying. Having these conversations is my way of coming to terms with my loss and of looking for ways to help me and you cope.

EMOTIONS GO UNDERGROUND, ELABORATE FUNERALS IN VOGUE - VICTORIAN ERA

SOMETIMES TO UNDERSTAND where we are now and how we got here, we have to go backward to where we had been. I believed I needed to return to the Victorian era to find out why we have such a hard time today dealing with our emotions. I also thought that while I was back in the Victorian era, that I might find the guidance I required to help me better understand my grief. I believed that folks from this era would have a set of instructions for me on how to deal with my grief. After all, they had rules and guidance for everything else ... why not also for how to handle death and grief? Surprisingly, there was mention of nineteenth-century mourning rituals and how they sufficed to help people meet the psychological needs of the bereaved. They structured the grieving process within a framework to reduce the terrifying aspects of death. This framework also rallied the support of family and friends as stated by Pat Jalland in her book *Death in the Victorian Family*. I uncovered rules and guidelines around funerals and these do not appear to have really changed much in modern society.

I confess that I am a lover of history, so it would only be fitting that I would look to this era for solace and comfort. To me, Victorian life was all about etiquette and rules for being in society. Numerous books were written to explain the rules, and young girls were sent to "finishing schools" to learn them. *The Queen & Cassell's Household Advice* appeared to be the "go-to" guide for all the rules. Although Victorian society as a whole was quite complex, I was unable to find a book which focused solely on emotions—quite possibly because Victorian society frowned upon open displays of emotions. Death in Victorian England was an elaborate affair and more focused on external things than internal ones.

Perhaps in my grief, I was romanticizing the notion of a family in mourning, of seeing them all together and withdrawing from society for a certain period of time. This was a period of great transition, but also one of solitude—an opportunity to do the inner work, or so I thought (although, I did not find anything to back this up). It was the importance of withdrawing and family connection that intrigued me. I wish that this was a ritual we held onto in modern society. A society that had an understanding of what was required at such times of grief and mourning for a person to adjust seemed to comfort me. Time spent away from work for a couple of weeks, perhaps, instead of the customary four days; that seemed more doable. For some people today there is no bereavement leave at all. Perhaps, that was the appeal to me—the opportunity to withdraw so that I could take time to truly mourn before jumping right back into the real world and trying to pick up the pieces of my life right away.

I continued to think of the Victorian times, which, to me, seemed to be a much simpler time despite all the rules. At least they gave guidance so that one knew what to do. You didn't have to guess your way through things. The mourning period seemed to be quite strict, especially for a widow. She was expected to withdraw herself from public appearances for a period of one year, out of respect for the deceased. I can't imagine how it would have worked in healing their emotions, as the Victorians were notorious for their "stiff upper lip." Emotions were to be held in and definitely not shown in public. How did they deal with them in the privacy of their own homes? Pat Jalland mentioned that women would write to a close friend about what they were experiencing. So, perhaps although they mourned alone, sharing their sorrows with others was what helped them heal. I discovered it was not all quite as I had imagined, but I did come away with a different understanding of the period. You, too, may enjoy a walk into the past.

The Victorians certainly had a healthy respect for death. They were not fearful of the way we modern folks appear to be. Death was more present in their lives, as people often died at home. The body of the deceased would be prepared and cared for in the parlour until the burial. Yes, parlours were built just for such occasions. Life expectancy in the Victorian era was between 40 and 52; so, many children were exposed to death from an early age and there were high rates of infant mortality. Families also lived in closer proximity to each other and could rely on their female relatives or neighbours to offer support during such times. They were more present and involved with death than we are in society today where death has become hidden and clinical. This has removed us further from the grief process, and people's views about death have changed just as much as the way people die today.

The study of death and bereavement in the past is intriguing, as it helps us understand the present, especially, in the context of modern society. Today the subject of death is avoided altogether. Scholars in the humanities have long recognized the need for the further study of death and grief in contemporary society. According to author Pierre Chaunu, every society is gauged and assesses itself in some way by its system of death. What does this mean for modern society with our death averseness and increasing need to remove rituals from our lives?

Grief's Abyss

Victorian Britain was a period of vast differences in attitudes between the upper and lower classes with respect to death and dying. The upper class could afford lavish funerals and take a year away from society. The lower classes had to get on with their lives to ensure their survival. They were the ones who were inflicted with the insults of a pauper's grave. This was a huge disgrace in Victorian England at the time. Evangelicalism helped to play a major role and the church had much influence on the family life. The family was seen as a shelter for moral and spiritual values. They shared a Christian belief that a family suffering together during a death would be reunited in heaven. Evangelicalism would, however, begin to wane in the last quarter of the nineteenth century, and traditions about death and immortality declined along with it.

The Victorian family was depicted as being claustrophobic and oppressive with its many rules about etiquette. It was assumed that because of their great piety their lives must have lacked joy and laughter. Proof exists, however, that the Evangelical family was actually quite cheerful. They just held their emotions in check for certain solemn occasions.

Emotional displays and the romanticised deathbed scenes commonly portrayed in Hollywood movies were much more common in the Edwardian period and during the early part of the Victorian era. However, the age of open emotional expression was already changing by the 1870s to 1880s. This decline was further accelerated by the opening of public schools. Thanks to public schools, the belief was born that it was not manly to cry. Men, therefore, were required to be reserved when dealing with grief. The Great War saw further attitudes about death beginning to change. New demographic patterns also emerged in the 1870s that had a significant impact on the history of death, especially, during the 1880s.

Another change was the rise of medical knowledge in Victorian England, particularly around pain control for terminally ill patients. This forced a change in how people viewed death. In the early and mid-Victorian period, a good Christian believed that death was divinely ordained. But with the medical use of opiates and alcohol to help with the pain, death became more about having a disease as opposed to being divinely ordained. A decline in faith came about with this new knowledge of disease even though there was still a limited cure rate. Early doctors could help alleviate the pain with opiates and alcohol for patients in their care. Thus the first palliative care physicians were born.

Further changes emerged with the events of World War I from 1914 to 1918. During this time, countless men, young and old, would die abroad and not be taken care of by their families or in their homes. They could no longer continue with their customs of deathbed farewells, burial, and mourning rituals.

The Victorian Grief Etiquette had two stages: full mourning and half mourning; each having its own set of rules.

Full mourning was directly from the time of death and would last one year for widows. They would wear full black attire and a weeping veil. These dark garments would be worn for one year and a day. Widowers could wear black cloaks or a dark suit with a black armband. Men, for obvious financial reasons, could continue their professional pursuits when they wished to—usually after a two-week period of mourning. They also did not have to adhere to the strict mourning periods set for women. After one year, a widow would enter into half mourning. This period was marked by wearing black silk instead of black crepe. The overall mourning period for a widow was two years. Mourning the death of a child would only be for one year. There were, however, different timeframes for mourning depending on the relationship to the deceased. Caskets were very ornate as were headstones. Cemeteries, as we know them today, those set in more park-like settings, were initiated by the Victorians for sanitary health concerns, which caused them to move away from churchyard burials.

We can thank the Victorians for their legacy of elaborate, expensive, and ornate funerals. It was important to them to ensure the deceased had a "proper burial" regardless of the cost ... even to the detriment of the family, who might end up living in hardship as a result. The ultimate disgrace would be to have a "pauper's grave."

Grief's Abyss

My need to understand what I would go through and what was in front of me was not readily available from any modern-day books I was reading. Instead, I experienced that with the passing of each day and month, the pain of grief did begin to subside; and after six months, life had begun to pick up its own rhythm once more. One year, and then two years went by before laughter and joy were once again daily occurrences; the black days of grief had finally lifted. It is interesting to note that the Victorian period of grief was two years for the widow and one year for the children. Did it count that I was the oldest daughter, taking care of everything for the widow (my mum)? Perhaps, my grief lasted longer because it had been put on hold to care for my mum.

For some, it is not so time driven; for others, they can become stuck cycling through the memories, clinging on to a life that was, fearful of letting it go, and moving into the future without the person.

Queen Victoria was one such person. She mourned her husband, Prince Albert, for 40 years. During those 40 years, she continued to dress in black.

Dear readers:

I did have a point by reflecting upon the above. We, as a society, have been conditioned since the Victorian times to hold onto our emotions as they are not welcome and it is not polite to cry, be angry, or show disappointment or upset in public. We have been conditioned by our parents to believe that big boys don't cry and that it is unmanly to do so. Girls didn't fare much better. If you want to cry, go to your room. Here, come and get a cookie or candy... just stop crying! They taught us this because their parents and many generations of parents before them taught them the same thing; for they were daughters and sons of that Victorian generation. Hence, we, as a society have learnt to disconnect from our emotions, and we have not been taught what to expect or how to support others in grief.

Grief it seems has its own timetable, and it is dependent upon us on how we cope and handle our mourning. Each one of us is different with our upbringing, beliefs and values, the relationship we had with the person, the circumstances, as well as our life experiences, all come into play.

The good news is that many of you will move through the grieving process in about two years. The one- to three-month period is the most devastating and painful time, but you are not out of the woods yet. You will along the way need to be mindful of the *firsts*. These are anniversaries, birthdays, special occasions during the year, or family celebrations where, for the first time, your loved one is no longer present. These firsts, at times, are extremely painful, but I didn't feel them as intensely as I did as those emotions felt during the first one to three months.

Don't cry because it's over, smile because it happened.

Dr. Seuss

THE NEED TO FIND OUT WHY

AT SOME POINT in your journey, you may decide you need to know more about the death and how the person died, especially if there was no prior medical concern. This again, is quite normal and is part of your putting the pieces back together to make sense of what has happened. This is all part of the reconstruction phase.

My dad had been seemingly OK. He was getting thinner, but Mum assured us that he was eating well. Perhaps he was just getting more frail because he was 88 and his life had gotten much smaller since he gave up driving due to failing eye sight. He had even stopped reading his beloved guitar music. He could no longer see the notes well enough to play and his memory, too, was failing; so much so, that he couldn't even remember how to play his guitar.

The week before he died, Dad had gone for a CT scan. He had fallen while out and about, thus the doctors were looking for potential causes. I recalled he had an appointment with the specialist coming up that

Grief's Abyss

I needed to now cancel. However, I decided to go anyway and speak to the doctor. I had called to explain that my father had died, asking if I could come and speak to the specialist. They agreed. The specialist showed me the CT scans. Dad had been full of cancer. He then said that it was a blessing in a way that he had died when he had so that he would not have to endure painful cancer treatments. Somehow knowing this new information put my mind at ease. Having someone to talk to about my father's death had helped me on so many levels. Now I had answers and something to be thankful for ... small mercies you could say.

Having this final piece of information had allowed me to free myself of lingering guilt—the guilt of being a former nurse and of "I should have known better" or "I could have, should have done more!"

Some may not be able to find out why their loved one died or what the actual cause of death was. For some people not knowing will not seem important, but for others, it could offer a sense of closure, as it did for me. Knowing the cause of death can sew things up so that the mind of the bereaved cannot go into the "I should have" mode. Healing can then begin with this sense of closure.

REFLECTIONS

1. What were your family's beliefs about death?

If you make a list, you can choose which ones you agree with and which ones you don't. You can also decide what you want to teach your children about death.

2. Were you included in family discussions about death?

Often families ignore chatting about death. How do you prefer to handle it in your family?

3. Did you attend many funerals when you were a child or young adult?

Do you recall what age you were when you attended your first funeral? What memories do you have of that experience? This will help you understand your thinking about death.

4. Did you know what to expect and how to behave prior to your loss?

If you did, you were one of the lucky ones. No one usually picks up a book to become educated in grief before the event. Most people prefer to avoid the subject.

5. Do you know everything that you need and want to know about your loved one's death, about why and how it occurred?

This is an opportunity to find out as much as you can about how the person died. This helps you to come to terms about the death and your mind can finally find peace.

CHAPTER 6

> In my deepest, darkest moments, what really got me through was a prayer. Sometimes my prayer was" "Help me." Sometimes a prayer was "Thank you." What I've discovered is that intimate connection and communication with my creator will always get me through because I know my support, my help, is just a prayer away.
>
> Iyanla Vanzant

FAITH IS EITHER LOST OR STRENGTHENED

IN THE MIDST OF our mourning, we at times, can become angry at God or whatever deity we pray to for allowing this to happen. The God of understanding no longer makes sense if he can let good people die. Thus, we can sometimes allow our faith in God and in life to die as well. We essentially cast ourselves adrift and find ourselves no longer tethered to our beliefs and our hopes for a better future. We may feel alone and as if no one cares, not even God. As we continue to berate and throw our anger in His direction, the more lost we seem to become. We continue to search, but for what? Our familiar life is gone. Our previous security and comfort are no longer there, and we cannot see our future. It all looks hopeless and empty. We can go into the dark night of the soul and move further into the forest, seeking that once familiar comfort.

What happens when we have no faith or beliefs in a God or higher power? We have perhaps placed our faith in the deceased, but they are no longer there. Our faith in ourselves to keep ourselves safe and protected has also been lost, as we are unable to continue with the simplest of tasks in our daily lives, we have lost interest, we no longer care what happens to ourselves or others. Our lives seem devoid of any comfort or solace; we are, in short, bereft. We look to the past and wait, but for what? To be rescued. But, by whom? Who do we expect to show up? How do we continue without our faith?

Those of us who were brought up with religion since childhood may find ourselves angry and enraged that God could let this happen. Perhaps we tried to bargain with God not to let this happen. When the opposite does happen, we are in turmoil. We often turn our backs on the one thing that has brought us comfort throughout our lives—God.

Those who are not religious likely do not go through the same turmoil, for they never had a connection to God in the first place. Some who were not previously religious may turn to God in their time of struggle for comfort and support.

Others may decide to turn their backs, rail against God, hurl abuse and rage at Him only to find their faith is eventually strengthened; because why would someone throw all this abuse at someone who did not exist? They do believe deep down that a God does exist.

I had lost my faith somewhere along the way as each loss chipped away at me. I had grown tired with the material world. I had achieved the American dream. Now what? A bigger and better house or car? Searching and looking into other world religions was my quest for years and my journey took me to some amazing places only to come full circle, right back to the faith of my childhood.

In a world that is forever changing, it is hope and faith that become our anchors so that we can have something permanent to hold on to.

ANNE E. DEBUTTE

DETOUR TO WISDOM TRADITIONS

TO GAIN AN understanding of our own beliefs and customs and what may be lacking, we often look to other cultures for enlightenment and answers. I began to search and to find the answers into why our Western culture was so averse to death. By hiding death, many of us, myself included, have had few opportunities to see how to deal with a death or receive any guidance from our tribal members, our parents, aunts and uncles, and our elders—our grandparents. My family unit had always been my parents and my sister. We moved 500 miles away from aunts and uncles, cousins, friends, and grandparents—my only teachers that could have guided and instructed me on death's intricacies. Instead, I was ill-prepared and floundered when death struck my family.

I like to see myself as a fairly intelligent and resourceful person. I have exceptional organizational skills and I love learning. I loved archaeology as a child and wanted to become an archaeologist to unearth secrets from the past. My childhood dreams were dashed when my mother informed me that the pyramids had already been discovered, and that she didn't think archaeology would be an easy journey for me. Easily dissuaded, it seems, until my 40s when dissatisfaction in my seemingly perfect life led me on my journey of discovery, I became my own archaeologist. I loved mining into the depths of my being for those beliefs that had me making poor choices and for inciting behaviours that allowed me to continually repeat mistakes. I would get the proverbial two-by-four across the head to wake me up. How many holes did I need to fall into before I would choose another path? My journey, my archaeological dig, fascinated me more and more as I delved deeper and deeper. My guides were endless courses and self-help books. So, when I was faced with the largest loss of my life, the death of my dad, the search once more began into the face of death with endless reading and researching the subject. It was not by chance my search led me eventually to read the *Healing Wisdom of Africa,* by Malidoma Patrice Somé. His work pierced my very soul. His words about his village, his tribe, and their beliefs had my heart soaring. His prose answered my prayers and filled me with hope. It is our modern upbringing, our Western death averseness or staunch need for individualisms that has allowed us to lose our connection with things that truly are important. We in the West have traded our souls from community to one of commercialism, growth, and greed. We have forgotten the other half of ourselves that needs connection and love, and have neglected the spiritual parts of our nature. We have forgotten why we exist and what our purpose is in this lifetime. We have disconnected from ourselves and from our ancestors. Let me explain.

In the village where Malidoma Patrice Somé grew up, his people, the Dagara tribe, believe that everyone is born with a purpose and this purpose must be known in order to ensure an integrated way of living. People ignorant of their purpose are like ships adrift in a hostile sea. The women in the village, through their rituals, discover the purpose of a baby prior to its birth. The baby is then given a name that declares and symbolizes his or her purpose. When that baby is born, it is the tribe's responsibility to remind the child throughout its life of its purpose so that he or she can integrate it into his or her being and not forget. Malidoma means "he who makes friends with the stranger." Malidoma was born in Africa, but was later sent to school in America. He had to learn how to make friends with strangers.

I have been searching for my purpose for years. My joke has always been: "I still don't know what I want to do when I grow up." I said this for years and also upon my retirement!

Let's go back to the Dagara tribe for a moment. I was so excited by their words and was sure their wisdom could teach us Westerners something. It is the community that helps to raise their children and not just the parents. Every adult could become a grandparent and mentor to the child. How many of us in the West have that kind of support? Often young parents are stressed out raising their children. They may have families, but so often members are scattered across continents. We lack the support of our community and tribe, and a partner.

We no longer revere and respect our elders or listen to their wisdom. Theirs is the wisdom of the ages brought down from their ancestors. If only we had eyes to see and ears to hear them. It is our elders that give us connection to our ancestors.

In Malidoma's village, when someone is sick or dies, it is not the individual who is sick; it is the entire village that is sick. The thought of individuals does not come into their thinking. It is the village's responsibility to support and help the person recover. When someone dies, the village stops everything to support those who are grieving. A ritual is undertaken and can go on for days to ensure everyone's grief is supported and dealt with. When everyone is done grieving, the ritual space is cleared and the village resumes everyday life. Grief for the Dagara tribe is a frequent occurrence; they cannot conceive of a community that does not cry. For them, crying can be an everyday occurrence. Malidoma states in his book that for us in the West, grief needs to be restored as a starting place for modern man and woman to find peace.

For indigenous Africans, emotions are sacred. For most of us in the West, emotions are an inconvenience and we want to banish them. How many of us are afraid of our emotions because we fear a loss of control if we give them free reign? Where would they lead us? We are afraid of making a spectacle of ourselves. I know that when a colleague at work asked me if I needed to talk about my dad's death and came over to give me a hug, I stepped back and looked at her horrified and stated with a resounding, "No, leave me be. I'll be OK," as I fought hard to regain my composure and control. I cannot imagine where I would have gone that day had I received her comfort. I feel I would have been inconsolable, would have made a fool of myself and, worst of all, what if others saw me grieving? What an amazing opportunity my colleague was presenting me—an opportunity for my grief to be accompanied and supported.

It was in reading the grief rituals of the Dagara tribe that I found my heart pushed and pulled. My heart yearned for such comfort. The thought of being supported in the way they support everyone in their tribe made me sad. How amazing it would be, I thought, if we in the West could learn to be that comfortable with our emotions and to understand them the way indigenous Africans do. They are the ones holding space for us to learn and how we, too, can integrate and remember the teachings of our ancestors. We were not always so stuck in this way; it is just that we have forgotten.

Grief's Abyss

Slowly we are seeing national outpourings of grief and how we are supported by strangers who have come together in such moments. I remember where I was when I heard about Princess Diana's tragic death. How many millions of people tuned in to watch her funeral on the television? The collective grief felt throughout the world was palpable. Her death touched so many people and brought the world closer in our collective grief. Then later the world was told of the passing of the beloved Mother Teresa. All the heads of states were at her funeral. It was heartbreaking to watch a massive outpouring of grief once again. And then came 9/11. Although it happened on American soil, it was an assault on the entire world. Our collective hearts were broken. I was working at the hospital on 9/11; the big TVs were brought into our conference room and left there for the staff to come and watch and get information as the events were unfolding in real time. It was such a surreal day, but it brought us together in America's national mourning. People spoke to strangers. They hugged one another and cried together. Planes were grounded as America shut down its borders. Towns where the planes were grounded came and offered help to the passengers stranded. The entire world, it seemed, dropped whatever it was doing to tune in. We were all with those families whose members had been or were still in the Twin Towers. Collective grief was felt once again. If we can do this for events such as these, why can't we allow ourselves to cry and be comforted by strangers when experiencing a death in the family?

In Malidoma's village, solemnity is discouraged because they believe it encourages withdrawal and suspends participation. They believe energy must flow, hence, their drums, their chanting, and singing their songs; all are designed to move the body to allow the emotions to be released. It is stillness that stops the flow. How then does our funeral ritual serve us? How solemn and still we all are during these times.

> **Community is the mirror that allows us to see our purpose and the school where we first learn the meaning of service.**
>
> **Malidoma Patrice Somé**

CUSTOMS AND RELIGIOUS PROTOCOLS

WE LIVE IN a time where society is represented by many cultures, and all bring with them the richness of their traditions. Many in the West lack a belief system and do not belong to any religious community. For them, when someone dies, conflict can arise over the deceased's wishes and those of relatives who are taking care of the funeral arrangements. Today there is a trend where people are opting for cremation without a formal funeral service. The ashes are then scattered or are kept in an urn. Some schools of thought believe that unless there is a formal ceremony or some sort of viewing of the body, there is no actual closure. I will chat more about this later on.

CHRISTIAN BELIEFS

CHRISTIANS TRUST that they will go to Heaven and be with God in the afterlife. For them, a funeral, although sad, tends to be a time of joy and remembrance.

Ministers will offer comfort and assistance to the family to help them cope with the death, and help them organize the funeral service. Friends will often send the family their sympathies in the form of cards and flowers.

Funeral—a Christian can be either buried or cremated, depending on his or her wishes. Funerals often take place in funeral homes. Both ceremonies—burial or cremation—may include hymns, readings, and prayers offered by the minister or the deceased's family and friends. If a burial is taking place, the casket is usually present in the room during the ceremony and is later carried out by pallbearers. Pallbearers are typically family members and close friends. During burial ceremonies, friends and family normally are able to view the body and say final goodbyes before the casket is closed. If the deceased has been cremated, then the ashes may be scattered, buried in a cemetery and marked with a gravestone, or kept in an urn.

After the funeral, it is customary to have refreshments and allow attendees to chat and share memories of the deceased. This is also an opportunity for family and friends to reach out and be of comfort to the deceased's family.

On special occasions, such as the deceased's birthday, on Christmas or an anniversary, flowers or other objects may be placed on the grave as a sign of respect and remembrance. Funeral homes may also hold special events on holidays such as Mother's or Father's Day so that families are able to continue celebrating their loved ones.

CATHOLIC BELIEFS

CATHOLICS BELIEVE in an afterlife and that once a person dies, he or she will see God face to face. If a person has committed an offence or crime and has not repented prior to death, then that person cannot enter Heaven.

When a person is close to death, the family or friends will ask for a priest to come and pray with the dying and the family. The priest will administer the Sacrament of the Anointing of the Sick. The soon-to-be-deceased will be anointed with holy oils and offered the Sacrament of Reconciliation and Holy Communion. The priest will then comfort the family and help them prepare for the funeral.

Funeral—the Catholic funeral rite is called the Order of Christian Funerals. Family and friends pray for the soul of the deceased and ask God to receive his or her soul into His eternal glory. The Vigil of the Deceased (a prayer service) is held the night before the funeral. On the day of the funeral, a Requiem Mass for the deceased is celebrated. The mass includes scripture, prayers, and hymns. Family and friends are invited to participate in the service.

At the grave or place of entombment, the Rite of Committal is celebrated. Family members and friends, along with the priest, pray once again for the deceased as they commit the body or cremated remains to the final resting place. The grave site will also be blessed.

THE JEWISH PRACTISE - SHIVA AND MOURNING

JUDAISM PROVIDES a structured approach to mourning with five stages. These stages guide the mourners through their loss and pain so that they can be eased back into the world of the living. It is their emotional, spiritual, and psychological health that is cared for.

This first stage is the pre-burial mourning, and this is the most intense period between the death and the burial. This stage is characterized by numbing, paralyzing grief. It is only the immediate family members who are concerned with the funeral and burial arrangements. No one should approach the family members at this time as they are inconsolable with grief and need to be on their own. Someone can stand close by for support but no words may be spoken.

The next two to three stages are referred to as sitting Shiva. Shiva begins after the burial and is observed for seven days. Mourners take a break from all routines and involvement in their day-to-day lives. They focus instead on the memory of the deceased in ways that will honour the person and his or her life. The family is supported and comforted by its extended family, close friends, and the community. Working is forbidden during this stage.

Those who visit the bereaved are there to be supportive, to visit, to listen, and not to place any burden on the family. Candles are lit and will burn from the time of the burial until the morning of the seventh day. Five candles are lit in accordance with the *Kabbalah,* and they represent the five levels of the soul and correspond to the stages of mourning. All mirrors and pictures in the house of mourning are covered during these seven days.

The family in mourning does not leave the Shiva house until the end of Shiva, on the morning of the seventh day. To be in public would force them to put on an inappropriate public face. Once Shiva ends on the seventh day, the family members may go back to their everyday lives.

The fourth stage occurs during the next 30 days and certain mourning practises must be followed, including not purchasing or wearing new clothes, not cutting one's hair, not enjoying music or entertainment, or participating in any joyous events.

The fifth stage takes place at the end of the first year, and it is only the person who has lost a parent that is still considered a mourner after the first 30 days. This is because psychologically and spiritually, our connection to our parents is the essential relationship that defines who we are. Therefore, the loss of a parent requires a longer adjustment period. This stage guides the bereaved into a deep state of gratitude for all that their parents gave and did for them throughout their lives.

BALINESE BELIEFS

THIS CREMATION STORY has its origins in the Hindu tradition and can differ from those practised in India. The whole community participates in the ceremony, and no expense is spared to ensure the rituals are performed. These rituals are undertaken to purify the deceased of earthly impurities and to allow his or her soul to enter the divine world of his or her ancestors. Funeral rites are conducted in stages. The soul is partially purified at the time of cremation. Full purification takes place through rituals conducted at the deceased person's home, after the funeral. Prior to cremation, the deceased is buried in the local cemetery as the family awaits a cremation date that is proclaimed by a priest. The family will inform the deceased of this in a special spiritual ceremony that is either conducted in the temple of death or at the cemetery where the cremation will take place.

A celebration lasting for three days is carried out prior to cremation. First the corpse is bathed in holy water. On the second day, offerings are made, such as the beautiful and colourful tall wooden funeral tower, which will be used to carry the deceased. On the third day, the body of the deceased is put inside the tower, which represents the universe. As the Balinese believe in reincarnation, the funeral is not supposed to be a sad occasion.

All traditions have, at their root, honouring and respecting of the deceased and support for his or her family.

REFLECTIONS

1 **Was your faith challenged after the death of a beloved family member?**

A death can certainly challenge your beliefs in many areas and, especially, your faith. What do you really believe in, or were you just going through the motions? It helps to have a sense of connection to something bigger than ourselves.

2 **Do you have a spiritual practise?**

It is universal that we each search for the meaning in life. Spiritual practise can be a great source of strength to human beings.

3 **Could we in the West benefit from adopting some of the ancient wisdoms of the East?**

After all, we all seek connections and relationships with one another. To give another human being support and comfort is what being compassionate really means.

CHAPTER 7

> There is no greater agony than bearing
> an untold story inside you.
>
> Maya Angelou

TELLING YOUR STORY AND BEING SUPPORTED

SOMETIMES WE wonder how we have survived thus far. Your loved one has died; your head is telling you this and it must be true for you have witnessed the funeral and watched as everyone paid their respects. But it is hard to truly understand, accept, and fully grasp what has occurred. Your heart is heavy with hurt; there is a belief and hope that any day you will wake up from this terrible nightmare and find out that it was just a dream, and that life will return to what it was before. Wishful thinking, you know, but there is that part of you that wants to not accept the cold, hard reality. The shock and numbness have worn off or are slowly receding at this point. You can now accept a little more of your new reality, but it is still not something you willingly embrace. Telling the story of what has occurred can slowly help you begin to accept your new life. This is how the head and heart begin to meet and the slow process of healing begins. This is mourning.

Yes, you think your friends and family members are going to become tired of hearing your story. You don't need to hear "It was his time" or "she's in a better place." This is not what you need right now, and these phrases are meaningless and without comfort to you. Instead, the person to whom you choose to tell your story needs to have patience and an understanding of what you need to do ... that person needs to realize you need to tell the story in order to heal and move on. It is OK to continue to speak of the deceased and to share your story until your head and heart are ready to accept the truth. It is also OK to tell your friend or family member what it is that you need from him or her. This is your opportunity to feel heard, appreciated, and accepted, and it allows the other person to be giving and there for you. This is truly a gift, for in the accepting of their support, you are opening yourself up to receiving, while the other is being allowed to give.

This is also an opportunity for you to share with others what the deceased meant to you and to celebrate his or her life. You are able to exclaim that this person was important to you and that you loved them and that they changed your life. This helps ensure that the deceased continues to live in your mind and in your heart in a loving way. This is how you will always remember the person and how you will be able to speak about them with love and joy. The pain will subside and will no longer bring up tears as you speak about the person. Sometime in the future, you will no longer feel pain and sadness, for this will be replaced with peace.

The other alternative to dealing with grief is to never mention the person's name. For some, it feels best to erase all traces of their life from memory so as not to cause too much pain and heartache. This, unfortunately, will only cause the heart to harden and deaden as you try to move on.

In the previous chapter, we looked at how a Jewish family is supported by its community for seven days after a death. The family members have an opportunity to tell and retell their story during these seven days. In the Dagara tribe's village, it is the responsibility of the entire village to grieve for the deceased. This allows for the release of all grief and pain.

For the Dagara, it takes three days until they feel complete and the ritual ends. These rituals descend from the wisdom of the ancients and have been carried down throughout the ages. They continue to do so perhaps because they know it is a process and one that helps the person and family move through their grief. This sharing of memories helps make the death a reality. It is this critical step that is missing in the West.

ROUNDABOUTS OF GRIEF

THE JOURNEY through grief is never straightforward, and many travelers heading this way will end up taking a wrong turn and have to double back. You may find the Roundabout of Grief difficult to navigate; you may be uncertain of which turn is yours. Guilt is one turn, but I don't recommend it. Nor do I recommend denial or anger. On this roundabout, there is a turn toward acceptance. Why wouldn't you head straight there?

Grief as has been mentioned is not straightforward and has many confusing twists and turns before it leaves you. Let us look at why you would turn toward guilt.

Guilt is a normal part of the mourning process, and it is natural that you would feel guilty about something you did or didn't do for your loved one prior to his or her death. You may feel guilty if you laugh or have fun too soon after the death of a loved one. Being happy seems like you are dishonouring the deceased's memory. They have died, so how can you possibly laugh or do something in your life that is fun? This can be acceptable in the very early days, but watch that this belief does not continue for months. Yes, it is sad, possibly even tragic, depending on how the person died. But it was his or her life that was lost, not yours. For you to allow yourself to die a little in this manner is a double tragedy. Think about if that person were here with you today. Would they want you to remain sad and grieving? Imagine what they would say to you if they could speak to you. I am sure you would find that this would not be the case. They would likely want you to continue living life to its fullest and to do all that you can to rediscover joy. Review why you believe this and how you can make peace with what has happened, so you can be released from guilt and from the feeling that you should not enjoy happy moments.

Anger, too, is part of the mourning process. At first, it is natural that you feel anger over the death. You loved this person and now they are no longer here. Imagine a small child having a beloved toy taken away. The child would certainly be angry. He or she may even throw a tantrum. Anger at the person who has died is also not uncommon, especially if your relationship with him or her was tumultuous or dysfunctional, and one you were hoping to fix before they passed away. You are angry because this cannot happen now. It is much easier to remain angry than to confront your anger and figure it out. Anger toward God or another higher power has already been discussed. It is always easier to blame an external power than to look inside ourselves for answers. Your anger keeps people and yourself from getting too close to what you really fear, and that is your pain. Remaining angry guarantees that you will not have to feel your pain. This will, however, help distract you from that roundabout until you are ready to confront your anger.

Denial is another part of the normal grieving process. Denial helps us absorb and take in only what we are capable of dealing with at the time. It often shows up upon news of the death. It is a defence mechanism, a safety value, if you like, because too much reality cannot be handled or processed by the brain and body all at once. It releases the information slowly so that the body and mind can adapt to the news. We have probably all seen someone who, when confronted with the news, faints, screams out "no," and denies it. Numbness can take over and the person can remain there for hours, days, or even weeks. Slowly the numbness wears off once the mind and body are able to accept more of the reality. Some people may remain stuck in denial for months and even years.

Widows and widowers, and those who have lost a baby or child, also tend to get stuck in denial. They may acknowledge that the person is dead, but a part of them expects or hopes that the person will return. This type of yearning can go on for years. When it does, life is kept in limbo. The bereaved's life becomes automated without the person. All traces of the person remain. Their rooms are kept intact with clothes still hanging neatly in the closet. Part of this is the bereaved person worrying that removing the clothing and other possessions would be disloyal, or would announce to the world that they didn't really care about the deceased person and are ready to forget him or her. Some part of the bereaved person cannot bear the pain of removing the deceased's possessions or changing the room around. That would signal that the person isn't coming back. The tragedy here is that the bereaved not only loses the deceased, but also loses any possibility of future relationships and intimacy.

It is not that they are unable to mourn, for they mourn only too well. It is that they cannot pull themselves out of the river of grief and get back to dry land. They lost a part of themselves when the person died, and they cannot find their place in the world anymore.

Guilt, anger, and denial circle around with no way out of them, for fear has taken over. Guilt lingers due to fears of being perceived as not having loved the person enough, or at all. The bereaved continue to beat themselves up over the things they should have done. It is as if they are forever punishing themselves. Anger arises whenever someone or something gets too close to the pain. The anger is a defence mechanism to keep all out, including fear. Denial is nothing short of the fear in having to face the world without that person. Marianne Williamson says, from her *Course in Miracles,* that there are only two real emotions, and those are fear and love. Fear surfaces in the absence of love.

What was that part of you that was lost when the person you loved died? For me, it felt like my safety and security had been taken away. Dad had always been there and now he wasn't. The child in me wanted her dad back, to love her unconditionally. Who would do this now? It was in my recognizing the fear I felt around this thought, and the heartache it caused, that made me want to run. Instead, I allowed myself to stop and feel the pain that had been covered up. I realized I would now have to do this for myself and not look to another for my security or unconditional love. Yes, he was my dad and had walked with me as I grew into womanhood. He was also so much more. It was my selfish, childish need to keep him here on earth that was causing me such pain. It was this realization that helped me grow up, and I could look back at my dad's death with acceptance. What was the quality of your love or your need? Now that this is lost, acknowledge it and allow it to take you down into the centre of your real pain and loss. Allow yourself to feel it and just be with it. It is in the understanding of this love that you will ultimately be able to allow yourself to heal. These emotions, our guilt, anger and denial, are all mechanisms to keep ourselves safe. They do a good job too, helping us avoid the true pain. Don't avoid this anymore. This is not what this pain is about; it is to help you transcend it and know you can. Let your love for the person help you heal; let it help you grow into the person you were meant to be. It is human to love and, in so doing, we are opening ourselves up, we are allowing and knowingly willing ourselves to risk the suffering that may occur if they leave us. Will you risk closing down instead of opening up? The only true way to move out of grief is through it. All other ways will keep you on the roundabout. Don't waste another second going around and around. Your life is precious, and it is waiting for you. With love comes acceptance and, with that, your journey can continue through the forest.

THE OLD HERMITAGE - ISOLATION

AS YOU TRAVEL through the forest of grief, you may find deep within the forest that you stumble upon the old hermitage. It is so welcoming that it can draw you in without your being aware. You need to be alone and to withdraw and that is understandable; but be aware of the dangers of staying away from others too long.

In the first couple of weeks, you will possibly feel overwhelmed with all the offers from family and friends. How many of us say, "If there is anything that I can do, please call me"? The weeks following a funeral are when you can feel most alone. There is nothing left to organize and everyone has left. The telephone seldom rings. You will find it helpful to identify friends or family members that you can call. It is good to have someone there for you to just talk to about the deceased. How you are truly feeling and any concerns or fears you may have, need to be vocalized and discussed. Doing so can help with your grieving process. It is time to tell your story and tell it often. It doesn't matter if you are concerned that if you start talking, you will not be able to stop yourself from crying and sobbing. This is the point. Being vulnerable in this way allows you to show someone else your authentic self and to let the social mask fall off. This is when you need to establish a connection to those family members and friends that you know you can count on for help and assistance. Grief is something you don't have to do alone and, in fact, it is recommended that you be supported in your grief, particularly during the initial stages. Yes, you will need time alone and it can be a good thing, but being alone for weeks on end is not. Be sure to reach out and don't be ashamed to ask for help. It is not a sign that you are weak. It is a sign that, although you may not know what you need in that moment, you do know you need company.

I didn't do any of this, for my family had all gone back to England, and my friends were busy with their own lives. I soon realized that I had no one to count on, not even my mum. We didn't want to upset each other, so we preferred not to talk about what had happened or how we were feeling. I began to isolate myself.

Your world has changed and has not yet started to reorganize itself. It is unfamiliar. Your new life doesn't seem real. Everyone else is moving on because nothing significant has happened in their lives. Your energy levels are low because going through the grief process is physically and emotionally exhausting; your interests in life may have taken a backseat or simply no longer call out to you. You can't be bothered with other people's energy and quick pace. Even calling people on the phone is a chore. This is perfectly normal in the beginning, so you may have to isolate yourself.

Isolation is not natural and can be dangerous; we are social beings. When we isolate ourselves, we create loneliness, fear, and animosity. This can lead to resentment and bitterness and even depression, because we are unable to talk about or share our pain. This can be harmful as we are not allowing ourselves to process our grief and may be instead turning to food, alcohol, or drugs to help us cope and to help numb the pain.

You need to be alone at times to organize and be with your own thinking without distraction. However, some may continue the isolation because of the belief that no one understands what you are going through or really cares. Depending on the cause of death, there may also be shame involved. When suicides occur, family members naturally want to hide away so as not to be judged and not to have their loved one judged either. There are many people in today's society who are alone, away from their friends and family with minimal support. This is an opportunity for action and not sitting at home. It is a time to find a support group, a counsellor, or to visit your parish priest, minister, or spiritual advisor. These are just a few ways of getting support for yourself. Perhaps you would like to contact us for support at http://www.reconnect-from-grief.com.

There is also the old saying that many of us will remember our parents or grandparents proclaiming: "Laugh and the whole world laughs with you; cry and you cry alone!" So, we oblige society and cry alone.

DISTRACTIONS FROM GRIEF

NO ONE willingly chooses to be with their pain. Most of us would much prefer to take a handful of painkillers and continue on with life pain free. Our lives are way too busy; we have designed them that way. Life is too short, so we fill it up with as many experiences, toys, and adventures as we can get our hands on. So, when a death occurs, it forces us to slow down, to stop and to put our lives on hold. It is natural that we would fight this slowing down. Our jobs are important to us. We get to feel important there, so why would we want to stop working? There are meetings to cancel or projects to put on hold and people to talk to. We can't let others down. It is all an inconvenience, or so we believe, and, thus, we push on.

The death of a loved one causes so much emotional turmoil and pain; we're constantly in distress, unable to think, sleep, or eat. We were so good before at organizing and keeping our lives flowing somewhat smoothly. Now, in the midst of this life-altering event, we can't remember what is on our agenda. Somehow our brain ceases to function or we don't seem to care. We finally give in, pop some more painkillers and sleeping pills, maybe have a few more glasses of wine with dinner, and continue with the never-ending tasks. Whatever we feel, we need to get us through this. We are, after all, looking for a way to stop this pain and we need to have control, so our routines continue on the same as before.

Little do we realize that by doing all this, we are actually prolonging our mourning. For some, this initial coping behaviour may take hold of us and keep us stuck for many months or years. It is OK to lean on a few of these props in the initial days. However, taking sleeping tablets or painkillers requires close monitoring by a medical physician so that you don't get addicted. This is classic denial. It isn't your fault you had never been taught how to deal with emotions—especially those around death. You may have seen caregivers deal this way or even observed this behavior in the movies. This, however, won't help and may even trap you, keeping you away from your important life.

Then there are others who will pick up their lives and not skip a beat. They move on and move through their days without effort. They have managed to integrate their loss well. For them, it seems easy. Perhaps they are in denial? However, there are people who have a natural ability to pull themselves up and show the world how resilient they are. They truly loved the person and they are not in denial; they have accepted the facts and are now taking action to move on. Researchers continue to study the coping mechanisms of resilient people. Dr. George Bonanno, in *The Other Side of Sadness,* writes that resilience is a normal state, and most people can tap into it at times of crisis. They do well and do not require counselling or medical advice.

Others may not get off that easily. For these are the ones who truly appear to have gotten their lives back together again. To them, they are "just fine" and life is "just great." We need to look more closely at these folks because they are the ones who are in classic denial. They cope by immersing themselves in work. On the surface, they appear to be fine. They may even take on extra projects, pushing themselves into more and more meetings. They go to work early and burn the midnight oil. These dear ones will eventually crash at some point. Our bodies are not built to behave like machines. We need rest, relaxation, and healthy food, not fast food grabbed from the cafe or vending machines. We also need family connection, fun, and laughter. Entrepreneur and writer, Arianna Huffington, can attest to the perils of life in the fast lane. She may not have been avoiding grief, but she did work herself to the point of exhaustion and ended up collapsing, hitting her head on the corner of her desk. She was found lying in a pool of blood. It was this incident that finally convinced Huffington to reevaluate her priorities.

It is so easy to postpone and avoid our grief. After all, we have been conditioned to avoid it since childhood. How many of us were given food to comfort, silence, and distract ourselves or to cover up our emotions? It is a learnt behaviour—a default mode. Many of us adults turn to alcohol, drugs, food, cigarettes, and more to numb ourselves and to provide the comfort we crave.

When grieving, it is a good idea to maintain your normal routine. However, you must take care not to use work as a means by which to avoid facing your emotions.

Although it is good to keep yourself busy, in the initial stages of mourning, your energy levels typically are low. Grieving and avoiding grieving both take a lot of energy. Keeping yourself in constant motion is not a good idea right now. There is always so much more to occupy your mind than dealing with feelings of grief. You can throw yourself into gym workouts, volunteer activities, cleaning, watching TV, shopping, and more. Any activity that has increased during this grief period should be examined as a possible distraction tactic.

It is important to continue doing things for yourself but only things you really like. Delegate or ask for help from others with the things you don't enjoy doing. The same applies to work; this isn't a time to be adding additional work to your schedule. Going to the gym is important but take care not to push yourself too hard. Cleaning? Well, who enjoys cleaning? I know my sister does and could be caught on her hands and knees washing the floors because cleaning helps her release her anger. People in grief can also be angry. This could be the new "in" strategy for them.

There is no right or wrong way to move through grief because everyone is different, and there are many factors in one's life that can hold them back. There are those codependency relationships or overly dependent relationships. An elderly widow may not be comfortable taking over the finances, as this was a job her husband always took care of. A widower may have no clue about grocery shopping or cooking. Who are they if they are not taking care of their partner or fixing something? This is your opportunity to review your beliefs, better understand how you cope, discover what you still need to mourn, figure out what isn't working or what is. The list is seemingly endless. One way to find out is to ask those who have travelled the path previously. They can advise you, so seek them out.

When your journey starts to make sense, you feel more comfortable and know where you are, the forest and the confusion of grief begin to recede. The forest becomes less dense, and you can see your way out. The path to a new existence lies ahead. Celebrate that you have made it this far! Your emotions are becoming more manageable and you are starting to engage in life once more.

REFLECTIONS

1 Have you told your story of grief often?

If you are unable to share your story or there is no one there to listen to you, check out online grief support groups as well as local support groups. Through them, you can meet new people and perhaps even make new friends who will be there for you after you have moved on from your loss.

2 What have you noticed yourself doing more of?

Sometimes our behaviours are subconscious, and we do them without being aware of them. We are in default mode. Being aware of your coping strategy can help you avoid getting addicted to negative behaviours.

3 What new healthy coping strategies can you adopt?

Establish new routines; celebrate small successes. Do things that recharge you; what activity makes you feel up? Balance activities such as household chores with something you love to do as well. Deal with negative thoughts - take time to write about them and then replace them with thoughts that uplift you. Practice gratitude, breathe and take time to laugh are just a few ideas.

CHAPTER 8

TURN! TURN! TURN!

To everything there is a season, and a time to every purpose under the heaven:
A time to be born, and a time to die; a time to plant, a time to reap that which is planted;
A time to kill, and a time to heal; a time to break down, and a time to build up;
A time to weep, and a time to laugh; a time to mourn, and a time to dance;
A time to cast away stones, and a time to gather stones together; a time to embrace, and a time to refrain from embracing;
A time to get, and a time to lose; a time to keep, and a time to cast away;
A time to rend, and a time to sew; a time to keep silence, and a time to speak;
A time to love, and a time to hate; a time of war, and a time of peace. I swear it's not too late.

Pete Seeger as taken from **The Book of Ecclesiastes**

SEASONS OF GRIEF

EACH SEASON in the year following the death of a loved one will elicit its own unique emotional response or not. When you look at each season, you will note that each one comes with a set of family celebrations and expectations. Wintertime finds us celebrating and singing about joy and love throughout the month of December. In February, Valentine's Day is all about love, romance and, if we're lucky, chocolate. Spring is a time of renewed hope, and, depending where you live, warmer temperatures and lighter nights. Summertime brings warmth, colorful blooms, vacation, and happy times at the cottage. We slip quietly into fall. The days are shorter, the leaves fall and the harvest is gathered as we celebrate Thanksgiving (North America). The change of seasons and traditional holidays are often difficult for a family in mourning. Many fear the holidays. Is it OK to mention our loss during a time of celebration?

Along with the seasons and holidays, we have birthdays, anniversaries, Father's/Mother's Day as well. In essence, the whole year is an emotional minefield waiting to explode.

During the first few months after the loss, you may find that it's the little things that cause you to become emotional, things like seeing a piece of clothing that belonged to your loved one, hearing a song that reminds you of that person, thinking of that person's favourite meal. Your emotions are percolating just under the surface it seems, because anything can trigger an outburst. Some people may find that these jags do lessen as the months go by; others may continue to experience the same number of episodes.

To help you cope, you might consider looking ahead at the upcoming year and noting all the dates that might trigger an outburst or be particularly challenging. In anticipating these dates, being prepared for them, may help. Just know that your emotions will surface, and, at times, they will feel as intense as they were on the day your loved one passed away. When you are aware of upcoming events, you and your family members can make arrangements and plan something special. This way, your emotions will not catch you off guard.

For me, the first difficult date came in rapid succession, three weeks after Dad died. You see, this would have been his 89th birthday. This was followed closely by Christmas—a time that is normally filled with warmth, laughter, and mirth. Thus, my family was hit right off the bat with two biggies. I wasn't fully aware that these dates would be triggers and wasn't prepared or prepped for how to confront them. My family did what we do best when faced with emotional situations—we each withdrew into ourselves because we didn't want to upset each other. I was also brought up with religion. My children were not as schooled in religion as I was, and thus, had no drive to visit the grave. Mum preferred to remember Dad as he was in their apartment and refused to visit the gravesite. Thus, I had to visit the grave alone.

This is a time to be with family, or by yourself, in quiet remembrance. Journaling, looking at photographs, and thinking of all the special moments, as well as the not-so special moments, with love, forgiveness, and gratitude can help. Yes, your emotions may return, but this is a good way to help yourself move through your own mourning.

Some people may find it helpful to create a new ritual, such as at a special family dinner, where everyone can speak about the deceased. Not mentioning the person and noticing the empty chair may be too sad. If you acknowledge the loss, it allows the family to mourn together.

Don't let fear of your emotions stop you from holding holiday events in remembrance of your loved one.

One woman I knew held a special marriage ceremony a few years after her husband's death. It was a ceremony to express gratitude to her deceased husband and put her marriage away. She was then able to move on to a new marriage with herself and announce her newfound independence. At the ceremony, she removed her wedding band and replaced it with a ring she had bought herself. She was essentially telling her new life that she was ready to welcome it in. In this year of firsts, you may not want to do anything but curl up on the couch or remain in bed. Don't let others guilt you into feeling that these actions are unacceptable. Perhaps, next year you will be more willing to create new memories and rituals around these events.

Some people might enjoy creating something symbolic to memorialize their loved one, such as a memory quilt crafted from his or her clothing, a painting of him or her, or a poem dedicated to him or her. Even planting a tree in the garden is a marvelous way to celebrate and remember your loved one. Really, it can be anything that which pleases you and is meaningful. Walks in nature, going to a favourite restaurant, or watching your loved one's favourite movie are also ways to pay tribute to him or her.

I am sharing these only to give you ideas. You may have another idea that is more appropriate for your loved one. Don't let your fear of your emotions or pain hold you back from what you feel you need to do. This is all part of the healing journey and is essential to the mourning process. It helps to sort out your memories and reconstruct your new life. Just know that with each passing year, the emotions will lessen and a time will come when you can speak about your beloved one with joy instead of tears and pain.

My ritual is to visit Dad's gravesite on special occasions and place flowers on it. He loved sitting in the garden and enjoyed gardening in England and, later, in Canada. Although he wasn't a trained gardener, the artist in him could appreciate the beauty in flowers and nature. He could spend solitary time watching the birds and listening to the wind rustling through the trees. I enjoy thinking of these moments as I arrange the flowers I brought to his grave. I talk to him as I do this simple task. It brings me a peace and calm that I had not experienced previously. It's my opportunity to leave and be "far from the madding crowd" (Thomas Hardy). My moment in time when connecting with the past is brought into the present.

Another ritual I created was a Prayer of Gratitude that I share during special family occasions. My family, like most modern-day families, is scattered throughout the world and not everyone can make it home for the holidays. Along with my dad, I also always include those who are absent in the prayer. This year is our second without his physical presence. While giving the prayer and expressing thanks, my voice was steady and clear. There were smiles at my inclusion. Mum smiled and thanked me. We have passed through our grief. Dad will forever be present and in our hearts.

At Christmas, I ordered a wreath for the gravesite just in case any family member or Mum wanted to visit. I hoped the wreath would be a comfort to them. It shows our love and remembrance of our most precious family member. He was a cherished husband, father, grandfather, and friend. Although not present in the physical world, Dad lives on.

> There are things that we don't want to happen
> but have to accept, things
> we don't want to know but have to learn,
> and people we can't live
> without but have to let go.
> Anonymous

THE IMPORTANCE OF RITUALS

RITUALS HAVE been conducted for as long as humans have inhabited Earth. Rituals, such as our daily morning routine, can provide predictability and comfort. For some, it is that first sip of morning coffee; for others, it may be cleansing our bodies and teeth; and others still may find comfort in their daily trip to the gym. The alarm clock rings, you jump out of bed, shower, dress, and jump into the car, ready for your morning commute, with a stop at the coffee shop perhaps. You then arrive at work, take the same route and park in the same spot. It is predictable and comfortable. But what happens if the power goes out and there is no morning coffee, no hot water for your shower, or the car won't start, or the bus doesn't show up? How do you cope when your routine is out of sync? Human beings prefer predictability, control, and a known outcome. Unfortunately, death will create the same unplanned unpredictability. When it occurs, even if it was expected, we are cast into turmoil. We feel powerless;

there is no control and no predictability; there is only fear. After a person dies, we move on to one of life's most challenging rituals—the funeral. It brings a sense of order to the chaos we have been thrown into. Funerals create a sense of predictability and control, and we know their outcome. They offer an opportunity to help us move toward accepting the loss of our loved one. We view the body and see it being lowered into the soil. Or, if a person has been cremated, we attend a memorial and the ashes are buried. Funerals and memorial services provide opportunities to connect with the community.

Rituals also allow us to connect with our memories of the deceased. This is why many therapists and authorities on the subject of death recommend establishing new rituals to celebrate the memory of the deceased. We are not taken aback by our grief when we recognize that it is an important, inevitable event in the journey of life. The grief we can feel during the first anniversary, birthday, or any family celebration or get-together is often a reminder that the person is no longer with us; and this can create strong emotions within us, emotions almost as intense as those experienced when the person first died. Being prepared and aware can help to bring predictability and a sense of control back. Perhaps by taking the day off work so as to be able to care for your emotions and be more present during your ritual is a good idea. This can help you and allow the process of mourning to continue in a healthy way. These rituals can be whatever brings you the most comfort and connection to the person who has died.

The act of a ritual and preparing for it can provide a sense of control and predictability. However, when you start on your ritual journey, suspend all judgment, and be open to whatever happens. Don't anticipate what will or will not occur; just allow yourself to experience whatever occurs. This may be hard for Westerners to do, but try it. You may be surprised by the outcome when you approach your ritual with a sense of openness. Rituals provide sacred space and a container for our thoughts and emotions. A healthy attitude allows us to not avoid challenges, but to confront them head on. As we move through our rituals, we are able to rejoin our community; we are among the survivors.

The purpose of rituals is twofold: to honour and to bring completion of one stage and welcome in the new one. Celebrating birthdays prepares us for the new year of life. Weddings symbolize leaving our individual life and joining with another human being to share two lives. A Bar Mitzvah is a Jewish celebration that welcomes a boy into manhood. The Native Americans sent their young boys out on a spirit quest. The tribe then welcomed them back into the community as men. Funerals are a way of honouring the dead by appreciating and celebrating their lives.

We share in these time-honoured traditions by being in community again. Rituals and ceremonies guide us through life's transitions. Mythologist Michael Mead describes three stages of tribal initiation that were performed as a way to guide tribe members through life's transitions. These include:

1. **Being isolated.**

2. **Having an ordeal or brush with death.**

3. **Being recognized and welcomed back into the tribe.**

In the West, we never seem to be welcomed back, so we continue to cycle through the first two states in our attempt to reach the third one.

I was introduced to Michael Mead and Sobonfu Somé by Karla McLaren in her book *Language of Emotions*. McLaren was invited to Somé's village, and it was there that she got to experience a three-day grief ritual. To me, it seems so sad that we have lost, or are quickly losing, the rituals that were passed down from our ancestors. Our society has become so fast-paced that even our funerals may become a thing of the past as more people opt for cremation and scatter their loved one's ashes without much pomp or circumstance. It is these rituals that bring us into our communities, our tribes, where we are supported and have our grief witnessed. We go through a trauma, the death of a loved one, and have to sort it all out ourselves with little or no support or understanding. It is as if we keep cycling back through the event, the trauma. We have to do this because we are losing the connection and understanding of the witnessing and being welcomed home, back into our tribe.

Grief's Abyss

I will share Sobonfu Somé's (she is Malidoma's Somé's wife) story with you to help illustrate my point. Sobonfu's name means ritual keeper. She was born in the heart of Africa, in a small country called Burkina Faso. Her people live in community, and rituals flow through their blood like oxygen. It wasn't until she came to study in the United States where she recognized that community and rituals were missing. It was then she recognized their importance to her life and. she began to search for her new community away from home.

> There is a deep longing among people
> in the West to connect with
> something bigger—with community and spirit.
>
> **Sobonfu Somé**

This was Sobonfu Somé's concern when she recognized her loss of community. It is all too easy to lose our way and continue to cycle through the first steps of the grieving process. Conducting rituals can assist us and help us through. There is the funeral or memorial service where in our grief, we are supported for a few hours by friends and family members. However, they all leave to go on with their lives. If you are not religious and do not belong to a church community, or are single with no close friends or family living nearby, you may be all alone to deal with your grief.

I have given several examples of rituals from other cultures to help explain—what I see now and know—is our human need for ritual and ceremony. It is so important to reach out and allow yourself to be comforted and receive support from others. It is not a sign of weakness.

LIVING WITH PURPOSE

CONGRATULATIONS! You are doing well. We have gone through some emotional chapters. I know, for I have gone through them with you. We are slowly climbing out of the abyss; we have faced our fears of the unknown. The unknown is now known, and those fears don't have the same hold any longer.

To continue on depends now on your attitude and beliefs. If you adopt an attitude something like the little train, "I think I can. I know I can," guess what? You will. We are what we believe our thoughts to be. I have shown you evidence of this in discussing Dr. Stephen Hawkins's work. If you think you can't survive the pain or you will be stuck in grief, then that is exactly what you will see. It is almost as if you will bring those very experiences toward you just to prove to yourself that you are right. In this case, wouldn't you rather be wrong?

We know our pain is there because we miss our loved one. The connection to them is lost; they are no longer there for us in whatever capacity we required of them. We know what will help us heal and how to connect to our memories through our rituals. Now what is left is to adopt a new attitude and know you will heal and move through your grief. You have all the tools now, and know what to expect.

To start to adopt a new attitude, action is required. In the initial stages of grief, it is difficult to even be active let alone do your daily chores. By starting each morning with the intention to do some task—no matter how small or big—that step will go a long way in keeping you moving in the right direction. These actions help to keep you anchored in the present and in your own life. Too often our thoughts are with the deceased, and there is no one taking care of us. It is as if we have left our bodies to roam around on their own and no one is at the wheel driving. No wonder we are confused; we do not have the energy to be in two places at those depths and take care of our lives.

I am not saying you, with your new attitude, will not still feel the sadness or pain at times. Of course you will. But once you can decide what it is you want or need in your life, you can visualize it and work toward it. This is how you move forward and jumpstart your new life. If you can't immediately see it or know exactly what you want, just begin. You know that you no longer want to stay in your pain and keep ruminating over and over again about it. You have done all that; it has served its purpose; it is now time to let that go. We have reviewed the past and have chosen to keep those memories that serve us well; letting go of those that no longer do. We can leave the past alone and concentrate on the present, for it is only in the now that we can create our future. Your future is yours now to create. Take time to examine your beliefs. Are they yours or ones that you've adopted from your family, schooling, or the like? When we are young, we soak up so much from our immediate family and authority figures in our lives. It is these moments of crisis that give us the opportunity to clean house and challenge our beliefs. We have seen from the Victorians how we have a lot of their beliefs when it comes to our emotions. What else do we believe? We now know this is not good and we understand the consequences of doing this. What else do we continually do because we have been taught to do it?

Review and challenge other beliefs that you may have because they have the power to run your life. Such beliefs lie deep within your subconscious mind. Now is the time to bring them to light. Once you do this, you can readily adopt new behaviours and perhaps new learning. If you believe that challenges are nothing more than opportunities, then you are on the right road to living your life with purpose. Your gift to your loved one is your ongoing happiness; don't doubt that he or she would not want that for you.

REFLECTIONS

1 **Have you mapped out your first year yet?**

In this way, you can make special arrangements—perhaps take the day off—when you know what event might upset you. Sometimes it isn't always the days or events that we think will be the hardest. It can be the birth of a grandchild, a wedding, or a totally unexpected moment. You may not be able to plan for all eventualities, but you can help lessen the pain for yourself by planning ahead.

2 **Are there new rituals that would be meaningful in your new life?**

Rituals are in our DNA. We need them. Who doesn't love a celebration? This, too, is a celebration, not only for your new life, but also to mark the ongoing connection with your loved one.

3 **What new attitudes and actions are you planning?**

Sometimes we need to look to the future and imagine what we would like to accomplish. Better still, imagine it is your eulogy. "What would you like others to say about you?"

Going through this exercise can help connect you to what you would really like to do with your life. You can see patterns of your values emerging. Imagine what everyone in your life might say. Don't be modest. Only your journal will see what you have written.

CHAPTER 9

The risk of love is loss, and the price of loss is grief. But the pain of grief is only a shadow when compared with the pain of never risking love.

Hilary Stanton Zunin

NEEDS OF GRIEF FOR HEALING

A FUNERAL STILL plays a large part in our Western culture, but I want to discuss why funerals are so important.

The Victorians had strict etiquette—rules for every aspect surrounding a death. The Victorian-bereaved person and family had no doubt what their roles were, and knew exactly what to do and when and how. But, did they understand on a deeper level the need for these customs? My dad had always wanted to be cremated and have his ashes scattered. He was all for no fuss and no funeral service. I was unsure why he changed his mind and wanted to be buried as my mother had requested; I never questioned his decision, but now, I do wonder what happened to change his mind.

I have shared in previous chapters how many cultures believe in burial and how others prefer cremation. It would appear that regardless of a culture's choice, it is the process and ceremony—which are attached to either of these rites—that give us comfort and assist with healing.

The first ritual for the family is the funeral and, regardless of what is decided, will have elements which have meaning for you and your family; ones that will help you to adjust to a new life without the deceased. Rituals are full of symbolic activities and meanings and, as such, these symbolic rituals have gone on for eons. They are a part of our DNA and bring us together—family and friend and community. The funeral is the final ritual for the deceased and a time to say goodbye. It is public; it is traditional and it has meaning. It is an opportunity to express your thoughts and feelings about death and the life of the deceased. You honour and celebrate the life of the deceased by sharing your collective stories and remembering the person and how his or her life gave meaning to yours. It not only encourages grief, but it also provides an opportunity for support to those who are mourning. It is an occasion that lets us see we are not alone. It appears that, as a society, we are losing this connection ritual as we opt out of burials and funerals for cremation, scattering the ashes, and continuing on with life. Cremations are fine; but they still should call for a meaningful service, or memorial—an opportunity for sharing and remembering.

To help us with our mourning, a funeral is the first step in the process. Having almost no ceremony—other than at the graveside (as was my dad's original wish)—would not have served my family well. We needed more. I had recognized the comfort we received with the gentle presence of the chaplain on that November morning. It was the same comfort that we would receive from others, the same feeling that we were not alone. The original pre-planned papers Dad had signed could not be found. I was then able to plan a different service from what Dad had wanted. I decided on having an open casket, a small visitation, and a service, although no hymns, just a eulogy given by the minister and my sister. This brought closure on one level, but a whole lot of pain on another. It was final; there is no denying that.

According to grief counsellor, Allan D. Wolfelt, Ph.D., and in his book *Understanding Your Grief,* along with his website www.griefworks.com—which elaborates further than what is outlined in his book—there are six needs that are central to healing grief. When these needs are met, the bereaved person is better able to move through and reconcile their grief.

The first need begins with the funeral. The funeral helps to acknowledge the reality of the death. This is the act of acknowledging intellectually the person has died. We either view the person in an open casket or we are witness to the casket being lowered into the ground.

The second need of mourning is when we can actively be with our pain and loss. This allows us to heal and not to run from the pain. Expressing our feelings and emotions and knowing it is safe for us to do so help. The funeral is where we come face to face with our feelings, perhaps for the first time. The funeral is also an event where we receive comfort and compassion. This is our public mourning.

Next, comes **the third need**, which is remembering the person—and this is the purpose of eulogies. Eulogies give us an opportunity to hear and share stories about the deceased person and reflect on his or her life. We move from having the person physically in our lives to having the person live in our memories. We will always cherish that person's memory and he or she will live on with love in our hearts.

The need to develop a new identity is mourning-**need number four**. We are so used to being a wife/husband, son/daughter, or parent. But when that person dies, we find we are no longer in whatever that role had been. I am no longer my father's daughter, and my mother is no longer a wife. Our roles changed the day my father died. The funeral is an open acceptance of your new role. People acknowledge you in this role and are still there for you. According to Dr. Wolfelt, when there is no funeral, there is no opportunity to acknowledge the change of roles, and this can leave us feeling abandoned. We often hear, "When so-and- so died, a part of me died, too," Dr. Wolfelt says this is a self-identity issue.

Our search for meaning is mourning-**need number five**. This need finds us asking many questions, such as why did my loved one have to die, why does it hurt so much, and what happens now. By asking these questions we get to think about about possible answers. However, and more importantly, the question, "Why should I go on living?" needs to be answered before we can determine how we will continue living without our loved one. A death can bring our own immortality to the surface. A funeral is an opportunity for us to find meaning in the life of the deceased so that we can determine the meaning of our own lives. Dr. Wolfelt writes that each funeral we attend is a dress rehearsal for our own.

The final and sixth need is to allow ourselves to receive support. Support is required for those mourning and the funeral is an opportunity for the bereaved to begin to get this support from family and friends. When there is no funeral, it is saying that we do not want to be supported. It is in receiving support that we allow ourselves to not feel so alone. Receiving physical support is one of the most critical aspects of a funeral.

I never understood why people attend the funerals of people they didn't personally know. Now I understand; it is to show support for the living. Grief needs to be supported. Grief is not a solo undertaking.

HELPING CHILDREN COPE

IT HAS BEEN my experience and belief, but then I'm no psychologist or psychiatrist, that children are capable of handling death and should not be left out of the process. If a parent is comfortable with death and their own emotions, then teaching their children and modelling how to deal with it are acts of kindness.

My mum was not comfortable with death or her emotions. It was her belief that there were enough bad things in the world, and children didn't need to know about them until a time when they were older and would be better able to deal with it. Pretty good thinking. What parent doesn't want to protect his or her children? However, I know from personal experience that I was ill-equipped to handle conflict. When bad things happened, I was clueless because I had never witnessed my parents going through difficult times. When I went through a divorce, I didn't know how to cope with the pain. All I could think of was running away from the situation and the feelings. Classic denial. Leave town, leave your job and country, and escape. Not a good idea because my problems and emotions followed me to my new country. I brought an additional suitcase with me without realizing it.

So when my dad died, I again didn't know how to cope. How many others can say the same thing? Yes, we learn by experiencing it, but boy, is it a cruel and hard way to do so. At the age of 10, my papa, died. My parents sat me down and shared the news. I was consoled with the words, "He is in Heaven and in a better place. He didn't have much of a life and he worked too hard." Wow, OK, he is in Heaven but poor Papa not having much of a life and working too hard." This made me sad and I cried because I recalled the last time that we'd seen him, and all I could remember was how mean I had been to him. What an opportunity I, and we as a family, would have had if we could have gone to his funeral. Yes, it was 500 miles away, but to me, in my sadness, I think it would have helped if we were there with other family members. I would have gotten to see how others in their grief coped. We could all have shared stories and, perhaps, I would have received comfort from others. Instead, I was left with poor Papa and the knowledge that his life was hard.

Then, when we lose a parent as an adult, it is even harder to cope because we don't have their guidance. No wonder I didn't deal well with my dad's death. I had had no real experience with coping with loss or with knowing what to expect in terms of the pain and powerful emotions that would rip through me and lead me into my abyss.

The best way to help children cope is to be open and honest with them and answer their questions, as appropriate, for their age and understanding. Children, regardless of their age, sense adults' emotions, and if they are not included when someone dies, they may well believe that they did something wrong. By including them and explaining why you are crying, you are helping to normalize the event for them. If a child senses you are crying and you stop suddenly and put on a brave face, this is modelling the notion that people should not cry in front of others. Children are so smart; they sense more than they perhaps understand. This is a perfect opportunity to share why you are upset and then reassure them that it is OK to feel sad and cry when we lose someone that we love.

Children will not grieve the same as adults do. Their grief may come out later. This is their body's way of not overloading them. When they do grieve, it may only last minutes and then they may move on to another activity. They can work out the grief through play. Just acknowledge that their feelings are OK and that it is good for them to let their emotions out. Give them extra hugs and show them they are loved by you as well as by other family members and friends.

> It takes a village to raise a child and it also takes a village to heal a bereaved child.
>
> **African Proverb**

Children need a supportive network. This can be composed of other family members as well as teachers and clergy. Give your child an opportunity to have grief timeouts; spend time with the child. Perhaps prepare yourself and purchase one of the many books out there for helping children grieve and read it to them when appropriate. Include the children in the funeral, burial, and memorial services, if they are willing to go. This helps them to see and understand that it is OK and normal to cry and be sad.

Younger children may not be able to understand that death is permanent, but it does help them participate with adults and they don't feel left out. Again, answer any questions the child has about the process. Children, especially younger ones, will often block out information they don't need; so much of the funeral process may not be remembered by the child. Try to keep the child's routine the same. During a crisis, it is important that routines don't change. Continually reassure the child that he or she is loved and safe and that his or her needs will be provided for.

This way, the next generation of children can grow up knowing how to handle their emotions and will be well-equipped with the next death of a family member. It never gets easy, because to love means we must eventually mourn.

LAUGHTER IN THE FACE OF ADVERSITY

WE NEVER KNOW whether laughter is appropriate at the time of a death, or even at or around the funeral. However, I experienced laughter at the most inappropriate times and will share it with you to show that at certain moments, our bodies need to be released from the depths of our grief. We need to be brought into a lighter state and it is OK. This is our emotions at their finest. Don't despair if it happens to you.

I was asked by the funeral home to bring clothes for my dad. This was a very emotional request and not at all anticipated. I would need to involve Mum. It upset me to think about, so I couldn't imagine how Mum would react. Finally I told her and together, we went through his clothes and chose a few of his favourites. I took the pieces we had picked out to the funeral home. I was just getting out of the car when I realized that we didn't put in any underpants! Oh, Dad would be flying commando! I couldn't help myself; the thought just flew into my head. I was sure Dad would have appreciated the humour. But, this was no time to be thinking such a thing and I didn't want to be laughing as I headed into the funeral home. I was embarrassed by my oversight and decided to share it with the funeral folks. They didn't seem to find it humorous. I apologized and explained that I often get silly when I'm upset or nervous. Again, no comforting response. I felt awful by now. What was the etiquette for grief, I wondered? Perhaps it was just me? Did I have a warped sense of humour? How could I laugh at a time when I needed to be solemn? Perhaps I needed to show some respect after all. Unfortunately for me, laughter popped up time and time again. It made me feel quite awful. Looking back, the laughter made me feel lighter for a few moments. It allowed me to forget the heaviness of the grief that I was experiencing.

> Grieve not, nor speak of me with tears,
> but laugh and
> talk of me as if I were beside you there.
>
> Isla Paschal Richardson

THE IMPORTANCE OF LAUGHTER

LAUGHTER IS HEALTHY. It can raise our vibration and help us feel lighter. It is OK to laugh even in times of death. Laughter can also be experienced when a person is feeling nervous and is the body's way of regulating and balancing itself. Moments of laughter can also bring us deeper into our tears. Didn't our mothers warn us if that we didn't stop laughing at once, we would really be in tears? However, laughter and humour allow us to cope. Laughter is a reminder that life must go on and eases our load. If we can laugh, we will somehow get through it.

Laughter has long been considered the best medicine for life's hard times and has a certain power that can lighten the mood and even turn a challenging day into an easier one. Even tears can be erased by a good laugh. It feels good if you can turn your tears of grief into tears of joy and merriment. A good laugh helps to lessen tensions and provides a bridge to moving on when the going gets tough. Laughter is contagious and spreads well to assist others in easing their mood.

> I saw Grief drinking a cup of sorrow and called out, "It tastes sweet does it not?"
>
> "You've caught me," Grief answered, "and you've ruined my business. How can I sell sorrow when you know it is a blessing?"
>
> Rumi

Western cultures certainly discourage laughter at times of death. The Balinese mourners smile and laugh. Hopi Indians encourage the bereaved to cry alone. Each culture has its own set of rules around grief.

Grieving is certainly no laughing matter, so if we do laugh at times, as I did, it feels as if we've broken some sacred rule. I would force myself to stop laughing. However, laughter is the body's natural way of helping us cope during stressful times in our lives.

It has been reported that grief affects the entire body and, when grieving, the immune system can actually be lowered. It is our laughter that helps to restore and balance the immune system once more. Researchers have also found those who can laugh during the grieving process are able to recover from grief much more easily than those who cannot. This may be due to either societal beliefs or because they genuinely cannot find anything to laugh about. I remember an episode on *Downton Abbey* (set in my beloved Victorian era) when Matthew Crawley was killed and the house was plunged into mourning. Many months later, his mother is having a hard time, as one would expect. When she is asked by Lady Grantham why she won't attend a dinner given by the family, she responds by saying she would feel too guilty having fun. To her, attending a dinner just didn't feel right. The wise matriarch, Lady Grantham, then states that it was Matthew who had lost his life, and he would want her to go on living. With these sage words, Mrs. Crawley decides after all to attend the dinner. How many times do we stop ourselves because we have some belief that it is not acceptable to laugh and have fun?

We all know that laughter is the best medicine, for when we laugh the body relaxes and our faces are changed by a wonderful smile. In fact, laughter is known to be a great workout. Science has determined that laughing one hundred times is equal to a 10-minute workout on a rowing machine or 15 minutes on an exercise bike. Laughter helps promote healing in the body by lowering blood pressure. When we laugh, scientists note there is a production of T-cells, and it is these cells that which destroy tumors and viruses. Laughter is also known to reduce the amount of stress hormones and helps us cope with our lives much better.

Research indicates that laughter should be a priority. It is healthy and a powerful coping-mechanism that can help to alleviate sadness and depression. Laughter provides the body with a reprieve from the stress that occurs during the grieving process.

If those in mourning are able to tell their stories about the deceased, it can start as something about them that will usually lead to some funny incident or situation. The person will usually then recall the seriousness and be in a better position to cope, because the laughter has raised their energy prior to reconnecting to their loss.

Giving ourselves permission to laugh is so important. We should have no guilt about laughing during this painful period. If you find it difficult to laugh, I would suggest watching a comedy or reading comics to increase your energy levels. Not in the mood for reading or watching movies? Then you can just start to chuckle to yourself and eventually you will start laughing.

Or better, still, why not enroll in laughter yoga? This can really assist in healing the emotional distress that is being experienced. It helps the grieving person connect not only with others, but it also helps the body release its stored-up emotions. Laughter yoga has the benefit of providing support and connection, as well as helping one get connected to the body. Laughter, coupled with deep breath work, helps change the mood state, helping the person see things differently. It can even give the person a different perspective on life.

REFLECTIONS

1) What part did the funeral play in helping you meet the six needs?

Write about each need and your experience of each one. Which one stood out for you?

2) What beliefs do people have about children and whether or not they should be made aware of a death in the family?

You will possibly find your beliefs are based on how your family chose to cope with death when you were a child. Do you agree or disagree with your family's approach?

3) Have you ever experienced laughter during a difficult situation?

Laughter, as we have seen, can help lighten our moods regardless of whether there has been a death. Have you ever thought about incorporating moments for laughter into your day?

4) Have ever you stopped yourself from going to events because you felt it would not be respectful to the deceased?

If you have, why? What were your beliefs?

CHAPTER 10

> I believe that imagination is stronger than knowledge—myth is more potent than history—dreams are more powerful than facts—hope always triumphs over experience—laughter is the cure for grief—love is stronger than death.
>
> Robert Fulghum

GRIEF'S GIFTS

ONE OF THE BIGGEST GIFTS of grief for me was personal growth. When I look back, I can see just how much I have grown in so many ways; becoming an adult may have been the biggest. Let me explain. When our parent is alive, no matter how old we are, we are still their child and, as such, we revert to children when we return home ... at least in our parents' eyes. Their beliefs remain ours. My dad would say to me, "Get a good job, Lass. Stay there, get a good pension and you will be set for life." This belief was deeply entrenched in my psyche, for I basically had lived my adult working life with that in mind. I had stayed in jobs that I had long outgrown because they were for stable companies. Even when I did finally try to take the plunge and leave, it was always hard to convince my dad that it was a good decision. I felt I needed his approval before I could hand in my resignation. He was always perplexed, wondering why I wanted to leave a steady job with a good salary. I would then remain in the job well past the expiration date. This made me dislike the job even more. I was reaching this point with my then-job just prior to his death. Once again, I stayed too long. I knew that I would be retiring soon, so why leave? Somehow, his death gave me permission to not only leave the job, but also to retire much sooner than I had planned. Life was suddenly too short to stay and suck it up for a few more dollars on my monthly pension. I was going to say yes to my life and live it the way I wanted to, doing things I love to do and having the time to do what I wanted. Yes, dearest Dad, you released me from the dream you had for me. It was fear that held you back from living your life to its fullest. I was not going to let fear hold me back from living mine that way. I can say that I finally grew up and became an adult. I no longer felt that I needed Dad's permission to do as I pleased. Not that I really needed it, but the child that I still was in his eyes and, therefore in mine, seemed to require his blessing.

My growth continued. Four days after I retired, I was luxuriously enjoying my morning coffee in my jammies and surfing the net. I saw an ad on the site I was on. It was an ad to join this academy, to become a grief coach and to possibly write a book. Well, both of these statements intrigued me. I knew that I would love to help others move through their grief and not get stuck or waste a precious minute of their lives longer than they needed to in grief. Here was a positive way in which I could gain the knowledge and tools that I had previously lacked and help others find their way to them as well. I had been contemplating writing a book on various subjects for years, but never seemed to have the time to make it happen. Now, here was a golden opportunity to do so. I signed up and six months later I decided to go for my certification in grief coaching. I committed myself to saying yes to life and seeing where it would take me.

Another wonderful gift that grief gave me is the opening of my heart. Previously, my heart was walled up like Fort Knox. No one could get really close to the real me. I had suffered way too many hurts, and with each one, came another layer of bricks to surround my wounded heart. However, when grief arrived, it shattered me and broke me in two. No wonder my life would never be the same with the loss of my dad. But, as I have learned, our lives can be rebuilt and we can become better versions of ourselves in the process. What did I do with my more open heart? Well, I became more compassionate and I am not so detached or rigid anymore. I am more open to others' hurts. I now have complete compassion for my elderly mother, whereas before, my responsibility for her was, to me, seen as a chore.

Compassion also changes the way we view our relationships. It allows us to be more generous and more giving of ourselves. With compassion, we have the ability to truly be present with our friends and family. My listening skills, too, have grown. I am no longer waiting for a pause in the conversation to get in what I want to say. I am much more interested in hearing what others have to say.

I also have a new sense of belonging because I have reconnected to family members, including my cousins, who tell me stories of our shared ancestors. We have so many that it is hard to keep up with them all and keep everyone straight. But, being with my relatives and laughing with them helps me to not feel so alone. I am no longer ashamed of my roots or my heritage, as I had been forced to do so as a child, when I was ridiculed and laughed at for speaking funny. Now I delight in hearing my family's soft Scottish brogue.

Connecting with others who have gone through similar losses is also enriching. There is nothing as healing as hearing someone say, "I can't imagine how you feel." To feel acknowledged and heard is so cathartic.

A major part of growing in grief is understanding; while in the midst of the changing landscape, you still have control over your future and you get to choose how you wish to respond when life gives you lemons. Just knowing that regardless of what happens, I now know how to cope. I can now tap into that resilience and pull it out to help me get through whatever comes my way. Mine was a baptism by fire you could say, and, like the Phoenix, I too, did rise from the ashes. Just know you can too.

Taking action and learning something new are two great gifts that can help you through your grief. Please share what plans you now have and what gifts you have received from journeying through grief at http://www.reconnect-from-grief.com.

GIVING HELPS GRIEF HEAL

DEATH HAS a way of putting us in touch with our own mortality. When we view it through the eyes of a mourner, we realize just how short life actually is. This review can cause you to take stock of your own life and question it. What do you want to do with the rest of your one, and only, precious life? How do you want to be remembered? For some, this is a wake-up call to move forward in action. Action is always good when we are coming through the grief process. Action moves us forward. For others, although they may feel their lives are over, they choose to focus inward and are just waiting for their own death to relieve them of their pain of loss. They, in a sense, die with the person in the grave. Again, it is a choice. Those who feel the impulse to move on with their lives will succeed. They will pick up the pieces. There is now a greater energy to invest in their own lives, dreams, and plans for the future. There is hope. You can see a glimmer of hope and it gets stronger with each passing day. You may not know when or how you will draw your last breath; however, you can make sure that whatever remaining time you have is filled with pleasurable activities that are meaningful to you.

In the beginning stages of our grief and mourning, it is OK to become hyper-focused on your own needs and to take care of yourself. Later, you will start thinking about giving help to others. Reaching out when our hearts have broken open and are full of compassion is healing for all parties—so much so that we are capable of giving to ourselves with a lot left over to give to others. Sanskrit's word for selfless service is *shiva*. Volunteer and move! The call to action and the impulse to evolve will pull you forward. It is using your pain and loss to help fuel you forward to give to others. And, in the giving, you will heal yourself. It is not a case of moving forward to care for others at your own expense or to escape your own grief work. It is more important to make your own self-care a priority. We, in the past, are so used to doing so much for our families or in our work that, at times, it takes grief to make us stop to rebuild ourselves and to get in touch with our own emotions and feelings once again. Grief has its own way in rebalancing us.

The gifts are many when you focus your attention on helping others. It is really quite selfish in its own right. Why? Because you can start to feel good about helping others and it, in turn, feeds your self confidence, which can help lessen your own grief.

Grief can trap and cage you in if you allow it to stay too long. It can create isolation and loneliness and lead to unhappiness. Giving to others is really the cure, the antidote to our own healing and happiness. We are human beings and, as such, we need others. We need human connection—not just electronic connection—to experience the whole person, the whole connection of being with someone in person.

By helping others who may be grieving, you will soon realize that you are indeed qualified to offer assistance and this, in turn, will increase your self confidence, for you have been initiated into the watery emotion of grief, you have been through the fire in the desert and have transmuted your pain into gold—your gift of giving to another. You have survived to tell the tale. You have more than survived; you have grown into a more holistic person. Your heart may still be tender, but it is full of compassion for others. So share your knowledge and willingness to be with another in their grief. No need for talking; just be and listen; and be a support. This is the greatest gift you can give to another person. Pass it on so that they, too, will become a giver in their own time. They will also receive all the gifts that grief has to offer. You are the role model for them so they will know they can move out of grief's cage, go through their own arid moments and, when ready, begin to pick up the pieces of their lives once more. They will then recreate their lives anew—ones full of hope and connection. It was, after all, connection that we lost. It is said that what we are most seeking or needing, we will get if we give it to another first.

St Frances of Assisi's prayer shows us how:

> Lord make me an instrument of thy peace
> Where there is hatred, let me sow love;
> Where there is injury, pardon;
> Where there is doubt, faith;
> Where there is darkness, light
> Where there is sadness, joy.
> O, divine Master, grant that I may not so much seek
> To be consoled as to console,
> To be understood as to understand,
> To be loved as to love;
> for it is in giving that we receive;
> It is in pardoning that we are pardoned;
> It is in dying to self that we are born to eternal life.

To explain how powerful our thoughts are, here is an example Dr. Hawkins gave of what these levels mean to the everyday world. He used Mahatma Gandhi, a 90-pound man as an example. He was someone with the power of his principle, "The intrinsic dignity of man and his right to freedom, sovereignty, and self determination." Calibrated according to Dr. Hawkins's theory, the principle registered as high as 700. Gandhi forbade all violence and, because he expressed his principle at 700, he was able to unite the will of the people and use it to overcome the British Empire. The British Empire represented force and Colonialism and this only calibrated at 175 and, as such, is founded in self-interest of the ruling country. The world was able to witness the power of selflessness versus the power of self-interest. The British Empire lost the battle. Dr. Hawkins concludes that whenever force meets power, force is eventually defeated. As you can see, if you were to use force to push through your ideas or agenda, how would it go? Yes, you may succeed, but it probably would not be easy; and will you be loved by those you have forced? What power will you put into action?

OUR LEGACY

A LEGACY is something we do in memory of another. Their death is the impetus for us to step out of our comfort zone and look to do something meaningful. It gives us purpose and passion for our lives. The young man who commits suicide due to a depression may cause his loved ones to open a clinic for others who are depressed or to raise funds to help others fighting the disease. Or they may go back to school to become a counsellor in order to gain a greater understanding of depression and ultimately to be of service. Or they may decide to volunteer at a clinic that helps others with depression. No matter how large or small the legacy, that person was the catalyst for you to use their memory to continue your learning and growth to help others so they won't have to experience or suffer what you have. There are countless trust funds that spring up out of grief.

Grief causes us to shrink when needed, but it is that shrinking in these quiet moments, almost as if a gestation is taking place, that a seed is planted. And it is growing within us, waiting for us to have done our work and to be ready to step outside and make a difference. We have a choice whether to stay stuck in the grief, holding onto our loved one's memory, or to put them down. It is their life that has been lost, not yours. Are you going to choose to take up the reins of your own life and make it the best one ever—a life filled with meaning? You don't need to put your own life on hold until you have more money or a better job or whatever you decide may hold you back. Once that idea, that little seed starts to grow and momentum begins, it is like a pull on your soul. It is evolution moving you, letting you know it is time to move on and begin your life again. Don't wait! Don't sabotage your life by staying in the past! Listen to that small voice and that perfect idea and find a way to make it happen. You will be so glad you did. Whether you decide to write a book, volunteer, or start a business to help others, know that it is the perfect thing at the perfect time. This is how a business is born. Make a resolution to go for whatever it is; you don't need to know exactly how to do it. People, things, or signs will magically appear to move you gently through the process and on to your goal. All you need to do is keep saying yes—yes to the life that is waiting for you.

Don't know how to do something? Google it. Join a Facebook group;

go to a Meet-Up; just get moving. Start as a volunteer in your chosen area. Go back to school; you are never too old to do so. I once met a courageous woman who lived in New York. She was a social worker who was getting her master's degree. This woman was in her 80s at the time and travelled from her home outside the city into Manhattan on a weekly basis to attend classes. The younger people in her classes loved her, looked out for her, and were her champions. She inspired them. She thrived and loved it.

Do you think you are too old to write a book? I recently attended a book launch for a woman who is in her 90s. These activities keep us going and give us purpose. There is a story in all of us waiting to be told. It doesn't have to be a book. It could be a blog or just gentle musings in your journal that perhaps one day can be turned into a book, or perhaps a set of poems that need a voice. Perhaps you are an artist in the making, and there is a masterpiece waiting to be let loose inside of you; anything that harnesses the forward momentum. Build and allow it to carry you safely from the shores of grief to the mountaintop of your precious life. You get to choose what's right for you.

My legacy to my dad is me becoming a certified Heartbreak to Happiness ® grief coach. I am setting up my business so that I continue to take this legacy further. I plan to place 10% of everything I earn from coaching into a trust fund so that it will build, and I can use these funds to be of further service to those in need in our community. I want to be a philanthropist.

What plans do you have? If you already know or are thinking of something, please post it on my Facebook page, https://www.facebook.com/ReconnectfromGrief. Let's see what ideas are percolating out there. We could start a forward movement. Come reconnect with your life and let me know what you are doing.

REFLECTIONS

1. What gifts have you received from going through the grieving process?

You may need to look back and see where you were at the time of the death and what you have experienced up until now to see what your growth has been. This is not meant to minimize the death, but to actually help you find meaning in it.

2. What legacy might be your gift to others?

It does not have to be anything grand. For example, it may be planting a garden. What would really excite you and be meaningful to you and your loved one? Creating something which is meaningful, so that it helps to restore your interest in life.

CHAPTER 11

> When we are no longer able to change a situation,
> we are challenged to change ourselves.
>
> Viktor Frankl

ACKNOWLEDGING AND FORGIVING

WE HAVE REACHED that part in our journey; for it is possibly time for you, too, to accept the person has died. If we can't yet accept it, we can at least acknowledge that it has happened and the person is not coming back. With acknowledgement we, too, must note we are being changed by grief. When we look back, which we will do in the next chapter, you will see just how much change and growth you have experienced. The old life you had, with its certain routines with your loved one, has now gone. That path has reached its end. With acknowledgement, you can now choose your new path and start to rebuild your life.

By not accepting our grief, we are, in fact, holding on to something that we cannot change. We become resistant. We hold on tighter and stop the natural flow of the grieving process. Instead of resisting it, we need to ask ourselves why we are avoiding it. Why and what purpose is this serving? It is in the asking where the answers can surface. The answer could be fear and guilt—fear of the future and what your life will be without the person, or guilt that you did not love the person enough because you associate moving on through grief with a lack of genuine love for the deceased. It is not the person you are letting go of; it is all the negative thinking that goes with holding on to the grief. Imagine if you will that it is you who has died. Would that person not want you to move on and find happiness and joy in your life once again? Of course, they would; so why should you feel guilty about trying to move past the sadness?

It is completely the opposite; by letting go, you are actually showing greater love. You have trust and faith that your loved one will live on in your memories and they will not be forgotten. Letting go is letting go of the resistance. This is what keeps us stuck and prevents us from growing. Evolution has made us this way. We need to adapt to our ever-changing environment or we will become extinct and die, too.

We need to learn to breathe through our pain and not resist it. An old adage says, "What we resist persists." How true it is. Birthing mothers receive instruction on how to breathe deeply and slowly and how to pant through the pain. When the contractions are at their strongest, the mother can use her breathing to go with each one and be in tune with the natural flow and rhythms of birth. To go against the flow with each contraction would only make them more painful. Just like a woman giving birth, if we resist the pain, it will persist and intensify. So, breathe through your resistance to find out what truly is holding you back.

Acceptance and letting go of the resistance are actually acts of surrender. You are no longer fighting the flow of wanting to swim upstream. You can become peaceful in that moment. The fight to hold on has ceased. The act of surrender can free up all that energy that was being used to hold on. You will feel lighter and freer in doing so. Will you try it?

Sometimes you can accept things, but, at times, there is still something holding you back. It is called forgiveness. During our lives, the person who died may have said or done something that hurt us and now that they have left, there is no opportunity for them to apologize or for us to forgive them. Maybe they did not apologize because they never realized they hurt us. I know for many of you, perhaps forgiving them will not be acceptable to you, but for you to have closure, know forgiveness is part of the healing process. It is much harder to forgive someone for a transgression than to ask for an apology. I can ask because I know what it feels like to finally forgive someone. It also feels amazing to apologize for something that I may have done or said to them. It is like wiping the slate clean. It removes any traces of old, stuck pain which can then free you.

Forgiveness is another way in which we can make peace with the past. We have all said or done things that we wish we had not. The good news is that it is never too late to forgive or apologize. The best part is that you never have to say it in person. By choosing to forgive another is another way of letting go of what you think should or should not have happened. It does not mean that you condone their behaviour or actions. It means that you are no longer going to remain a victim—a victim to your thoughts or beliefs. Forgiveness is a decision to let go of anger, resentment, and thoughts of revenge. Forgiveness can assist you in not holding on. For holding on to grudges can lead to strokes, kidney disease, heart failure and even death.

I got to see this firsthand. My dad held onto grudges. He had kidney problems and did die of heart failure and cancer. For that reason alone, I am choosing to forgive on a daily basis!

I am using the Hawaiian Forgiveness Prayer Ho'oponopono. For more information on this simple prayer's power, please see Joe Vitale's book that he co-authored with Dr. Ihaleakala Hew Len called *Zero Limits*.

There are four phases to it:

> I'm sorry
> Please forgive me
> Thank you
> I love you

You can say them in any order, but Vitale believes in saying them silently to the Divine (of your understanding) is the best way.

Grief's Abyss

Perhaps if Dad had realized the powerful hold his grudges had on him and the damage they were doing to his body, he may have opted to forgive everyone. Again, do you want to be right or be happy?

After forgiveness, you can open up and be ready for your goodbyes. I felt ready to do this on the first anniversary of my father's death. This was how I did it. I have other ways to help you, but first let me share this:

Around the time of the first-year anniversary of my dad's passing, I decided that I needed to get away and go on a retreat. I booked the date, thinking I was going for *me*. I was in a way, but I didn't realize I would be there on the first anniversary of my dad's death. During my time at Grey Heron, cocooned in the nest, as it were, I gave into and allowed my mourning to continue— which it did— unhindered by the business of life.

To help me move through and then on, my wise friend knew just what I needed. She instructed me to draw whatever I felt moved or guided to draw. She put on some music and left me alone. At times, classical or jazz pieces would play and the tears would gently fall. This was the music of my childhood. Sitting there, listening to the music and drawing, felt like I was honouring Dad. I was connecting to him through the music and art. And in doing so, it was allowing me to accept the loss and process the grief that I had delayed. The process lasted about an hour. During that time, I allowed the tears to flow uninterrupted. When my picture was finally complete, my body ached and I needed to move and walk. I went outside and headed to the ravine that is just behind the house. To be in nature and near the water was so freeing and healing. I pondered grief's process and what was longing to be free, and what needed to come in. The artwork and music had done their job. Nature was spreading her balm and healing my grieving heart. It was fall; the trees had lost their leaves; the grass was turning from lush green to a muted brown. Most of the summer plants had given up with only a few brave ones still showing their colour. The air was cooler; there was no sun to warm us. The day had a grey stillness that matched my mood.

The activity around the pond captured my attention. The geese had been content to swim and wander when I had passed by them before, but were now practising and warming up for their flight to warmer climates;

the plants too were settling in for their long-awaited sleep getting ready for their appearance the following spring.

I, too, was falling in with this rhythm of nature, and thought what dies away is never truly dead. The plants live on ready for the next season. A part of me had died; however, that spark was still there and like the approach of winter, it had just gone dormant.

Recognizing this gave me renewed joy and hope. I had space now—a space in which to welcome in the new. I said my goodbye and let Dad go. I crossed back over the bridge. As I did so, the geese took flight. I looked up and stared at them in wonder. Bye, Dad. I returned to the house in true acceptance.

A YEAR IN REVIEW

The first three months after a death are certainly the toughest to go through. The shock and numbness have worn off, leaving full mourning in their place. This is about the right time to seek a support group or coaching and give your family and friends a break. After all the planning for the funeral has taken place, the person's affairs usually need to be put in order. Trips to the lawyer, the bank, financial planner, or realtor, if there is a house to be sold, all need to be made. Closing down an estate and advising others of the death will require letters and proof of death. All of this is time-consuming and keeps your thoughts firmly on your loss. There are just so many things to take care of.

Each task brings you back to the death, and mourning starts anew. You will, of course, have your own life and routines to pick up and continue. ... This is definitely a time to simplify your life as much as possible and not take on anything else. You simply won't have the energy to do so. For many, clearing out closets and rearranging the furniture are things that they want to do right away. But these are tasks that can be put on hold until all the other, more pressing affairs are taken care of. There will be time soon enough to do all that. Time can move fast or slow

Grief's Abyss

for you at this point. For me, time was in hyper-drive. There was never enough time to get accomplished what I needed to do. My primary goal was to finish closing off Dad's estate. For my mum, I am sure that it was the other way around. Time likely slowed down for her. She was suddenly without her companion and friend. Her days seemed to have suddenly lost their meaning. Mum would wander around her apartment and slowly sort through some of Dad's things. Some days, she was able to accomplish a great deal. Other days found her lost in memories of each item she touched. Shredding old bank papers or any potentially important, but past their prime letters, seemed to give my mum a sense of accomplishment. Whenever I would call her, it seemed that this was what she was doing. This seemed to go on for months, but I never questioned her about it. It gave her purpose during this trying time.

She decided to remain in her apartment right after my dad died. About six weeks later, she called to say that she would like to move into a new and smaller apartment, perhaps in the same building. I froze because I couldn't imagine taking on the task of moving her. I put her off by telling her something smaller may actually cost much more. Why not stay and continue to enjoy her view of the river? So she did and I breathed a sigh of relief. It is never a good thing to make decisions this soon. Those who are grieving do not have the energy yet to accomplish such monumental tasks, and decisions that are made under duress may not be good ones.

Medical research indicates that six to nine months after a death, those who are grieving are more susceptible to disease. People are physically vulnerable after a major loss. Your overall mood and energy are low and this affects your immune system. Grief's effects are not just emotional; there can be many physical symptoms as well. Seeing your medical doctor may be good, preventative medicine.

By April, Mum was showing signs of depression and a checkup with her doctor revealed that she had pneumonia. Antibiotics were prescribed. The second chest X-ray showed worrying signs, and she was sent to see a consultant. She was diagnosed with lung cancer. To cheer her up, her granddaughter returned to Ottawa. Between us, we agreed that her apartment needed a new look—out with her old living room furniture and in with the new. Mum and I would then spend many days together going through old photos to make our Family Wall of Fame, she called it.

Moving on for me took a different path. Although I was no longer in grief's turbulence, I had put my mourning on hold, especially now, with Mum's diagnosis. The family braced itself once more for whatever lay ahead. The diagnosis clutched at our tender and still unhealed hearts as we tried to remain strong for Mum.

I knew what we were being asked to face. How could life be so cruel? Would we lose our mother also, and so quickly, after our father? We were still mourning Dad. How would we fare with another death so soon? Somehow, from deep within, I found my strength to push on. I was certain I knew what lay in front of us. A friend's mother had been diagnosed six months before. Her mother had sadly died while mine survived. I put it down to the fact that Mum never truly accepted that she had cancer. Each day, we would talk to her and each day she would ask, "Where and why are we going there?" "Mum, you have lung cancer," we would remind her. "I do? Oh my," was all she would say.

Perhaps this lack of acceptance is just what a patient needs. She never once got agitated or berated the fact—just a quiet acceptance each time we gently reminded her. In her mind, she was healthy because she had no pain and didn't know what all the fuss was about. Of course, we never shared with her our concerns. Death was not a subject we could readily discuss with her.

In reality, I ended up the one not doing well. Life for me was tough on so many accounts. I had, in a sense, abandoned myself during all of this. I had put my emotions on hold to survive. I had given me up. I was so unhappy and just could not rally this time. I was indeed experiencing what I called the flatland, where everything is the same and no changes have been seen yet. I felt that I was headed into depression. I was eventually diagnosed with pneumonia. I turned to my self-help books for answers. I picked up *Heal Your Body,* by Louise Hay and looked up pneumonia. It did not surprise me that under the heading of pneumonia it said, "Desperate. Tired of life. Emotional wounds that are not allowed to heal." Note to self: I needed rest to heal. I had essentially halted my grieving process so that I could take care of our family's next crisis.

It was just after this when I decided that I needed to go to Grey Heron for comfort, compassion, empathy, and what the British call "Tea and Sympathy." I would go there to get my energy tanks refilled and come back refreshed, I hoped.

We, fortunately, pulled through this, too, and are grateful that Mum remains healthy. Her body is intact, but her memory is now slipping. Alzheimer's Disease is our next challenge.

I recognized that I had just come through the flatland; it is desert-like, dry and arid. There are no tears and no feelings. My heart felt encased somehow. It was a place where there was no life, no joy, and everything seemed tedious. I was just going through the motions. My life was being recreated in ways that I could never imagine. It just hadn't arrived yet. I needed hope and purpose to help me, and move me along my path and continued journey. My previous life had been shattered; the connection with Dad ripped away. My heart had not yet fully healed, but I was no longer in intense pain. It was just that the joy had been sucked out of me, and I was searching for something else to come in and fill the hole—something to give my life meaning again.

My heart needed the comfort of knowing and accepting that whatever feelings arose, were normal and that I was not going crazy. But, grief isn't something you can package into a tidy box and discard after a specific time. There is no throwing off your black clothes after the year is up. Today, we experience death, the funeral, and life continues. There is no room for messy emotions in public places, and certainly not in the workforce. These beliefs are from a bygone era. Perhaps the pendulum will swing back again and our children will raise their children with more awareness and understanding of the importance of emotions. Perhaps they will teach their children about death and funerals and present them as normal parts of life and not something to be fearful of. Death is, of course, an inevitable part of the circle of life.

REFLECTIONS

1) What are you planning to accept?

It is being conscious of what you are thinking and constantly refocusing on where you are putting your attention that will gradually allow you to accept the situation. Recognizing that the unwanted thoughts are all part of the grieving process can help you. Focus your attention instead on positive thoughts. You are in charge of what you allow your mind to focus on. You have a choice of what attitude, thoughts, and emotions you will allow to dwell in your mind.

2) What are you willing to let go of?

When you can focus on the end result of where you would like to be in, say, six months to a year, it helps to move you out of grief and toward healing. Any thoughts that don't help move you in that direction should be banished. Pay attention to your negative thoughts and emotions and make a list of them. You can then decide what needs to be tossed and what should be kept.

3) What do you need to forgive?

Are there things that you wish you hadn't said to the person who died? Conversely, are there things that you wish they could apologize to you for? Make a list of both and use Dr. Hew Len's powerful but simple forgiveness prayer. It will help you to clean up any unfinished business you may have with the deceased.

CHAPTER 12

> Here is the test to find whether
> your mission on Earth is finished.
>
> If you're alive, it isn't.
>
> Richard Bach

FINDING HOPE AND JOY

HAVE YOU EVER NOTED how after a good cry, some of the heaviness and sadness that have built up disappear and in their place there is now hope and joy? In his book, *The Healing Wisdom of Africa,* Malidoma Somé writes that, in his village, the villagers gauge the amount of grief that has built up in themselves by judging the amount of their joy. When emotion has been fully unloaded, the rush of joy that fills you up can last for days or weeks. When that feeling of joy subsides, grief is again building, and will soon require another release. Isn't that an amazing reason to do your grief work and not put it off or run from your emotions?

Finding hope and joy, it all starts with gratitude for where you are in the moment. I recall an amazing story of a young man who lost his job and was wondering what he would do. He decided that he no longer wanted to feel powerless, so he began to find ways to be grateful. He started to blog about them and, before he knew it, he had a best-selling book. He could have become bitter and allowed it to paralyze his spirit.

Grief's Abyss

Life is full of ups and downs. Take out a piece of paper and draw a horizontal line across the middle. Make a timeline of your life with the person you have lost. Mark down each good and bad event in chronological order along with your age when it took place. Then go back and draw a vertical line from each event. For negative events, draw the line below the horizontal one. For positive events, draw a line above the horizontal one. Then join the events, noting the patterns. Your life line will dip and flow just as most of ours do. When life is good, we are happy and not necessarily drawn to make changes or seek additional learning. So, it is in the challenging times that we learn and grow the most. To learn more about this, read *The Grief Recovery Handbook* by John W. Hames and Russell Friedman

We tend to like our lives the way they are. Change can be uncomfortable, but it is necessary if we are to grow and evolve. Let this event be a catalyst for self-growth. Find gratitude and practise it daily. With the practise of gratitude, you will find happiness return to your life more and more. Yes, there will be sad times and these may continue for many more years. But, these will not have the same devastating effect in taking you down into the abyss. You will have moved through that and, with your practise of gratitude and happiness to fill you up, you will find you are much more able to cope with those moments and use that energy to move on.

Happiness is not the size of our paycheck, home, or cars. Happiness arises out of a sense of wonder and of good things to come. Happiness looks to the future. As adults, we have lost our ability to be spontaneously happy, as we had had as children. Just watch the determination in a child's face as they build sandcastles for hours; the planning and the fetching of water for the moat. Note how long this endeavour takes and how serious they go about it. Then someone suggests jumping on it and knocking it down. This then becomes a fun game, and they shout "Yes, let's do that," with glee and enjoyment as the hours of planning come crashing down, destroying the sandcastle. How many of us celebrate our accomplishments with such glee? It is time to allow ourselves to be silly, hopeful, and happy just because. We don't need a reason to be happy.

Think that you don't have anything to feel happy about? Try running up your stairs a few times; be that child for a moment and jump from the last few steps. Skipping in the house is also OK; no one is watching. That is sure to put a smile on your face and lighten your mood. Happiness comes in different forms, and it doesn't have to cost us anything. Just like finding things to be grateful for; notice those things that make you feel happy. The more you notice them, the more they will just keep on flowing toward you. This is a benevolent universe, and how we view it is a choice we make.

The sun is always shining above the clouds, and we can always find that silver lining.

ROAD TO THE RIVER OF LIFE

OUR JOURNEY is nearing its end; the climb back up has been steep. Some may have gotten lost along the way. Some may have grown weary and headed back. Others may have gotten discombobulated on the roundabouts—those roundabouts are tricky, but well worth navigating. We may just need to circle them a few times until we find our bearings and decide upon the new direction in which to head. The journey through those flatlands, where life seems to go on and on forever, nothing seems the same, but then, nothing seems to have changed either. We move on and struggle through, for we can see the mountains in front of us. The only way through the mountains is up. Just as with grief, the only way, is to go through it and rise up. It is so well worth the trip because on the top, we can see just where we have been and we can congratulate ourselves on moving forward and digging deep into our resilience. Now we are almost to the top. We can see everyone waiting there to welcome us back; our hero's and shero's journeys are almost complete. We are much wiser than before we started, for we know it is the death of our loved one that has caused us to head out on own hero's and shero's journey. As we know from Michael Meads's three stages of tribal initiation, going through grief has been ours.

1. **Our grief isolates us.** In doing so, we can return to our past and sift through the memories. This is how we make sense of it all. We can review who the person was and what he or she meant to us. When I lost my dad, I was no longer his daughter. It took time for that to filter through. It was in the stillness that I was able to make sense of my place in the world without his presence. I was able to answer the question, "Who am I now?"

   Whatever the nature of your relationship with your father, whether it was good or bad or downright ugly, fathers are the first men in our lives. They are the ones who were there to show us how to love. If, like me, your father was distant, you may spend your life attempting to be validated from other men—boyfriends and husbands. Our dads were our role models, whether we like it or not. Fathers are the root of the family; they are supposed to keep the family safe and often were the sole breadwinners (well, in the 50s). Our fathers, if they have done their job well, give us our sense of safety and stability. They are the home providers, the doers; the ones who help shape our personalities and teach us how to cope with life. We will either want to marry someone with our father's characteristic or we will spend a life time running away from men like them, for these are character traits that we despise. Dad was always at home; he never strayed far. His family was his life. He was a rather solitary man and enjoyed his own company. Playing his guitar in his bedroom was one of his favourite distractions. Rarely would he share his playing, even when we all pleaded. He could be moody and a man of few words. I can't say that I miss our lively debates because we never had any. I just knew he was there, solid, dependable, and ready to help me whenever I needed him. We had a relationship of mutual respect. He once had been a good playmate in my childhood and could be relied upon to read me countless stories. As I got older and my interests took me away from home, I never really looked back. Dad was Dad until he could no longer drive and relied on me to take him to his doctors' appointments, which became many in the latter part of his life. I was there as his support. The tables were reversed.

So, who am I now that I am no longer my father's daughter? I am still a wife, a mother, and my mother's daughter. I still have my place, but with Dad's death, the stability of my world has been rocked and his support, love, and approval are lost in some ways. This was how my friend described her dad's death. She saw him as the roots of her family. Thus, when he died, she felt that the family's roots had been ripped out. Here, the mother was the heart of the family. My friend has lost both her parents now and although she is an adult, still feels she and her siblings are orphans.

The image of a mighty oak tree came to me as she described her feelings. A strong wind had felled the mighty oak, and its roots lay exposed. Below there was a huge hole where the tree had once stood. This was a powerful analogy. With our parents' deaths, we have a huge hole in our hearts that needs to be filled and healed. No wonder there is such immense pain. This is the wound, the trauma that we suffer.

I had to grow up suddenly and become the adult-child my body showed me to be.

2. **We are often faced with our own immortality.** Dad was the connection to our ancestors, the men and women in our lineage. His presence connected me to them. Now, that too, is gone and I am next in line. I'm the connection for my children to all those generations that came before. There will be no more stories from his boyhood, no more war time stories of air raids and shelters, no tales of his loves and fears ... just fleeting memories in my mind of what he said and these, too, will slip from my memory one day.

With Dad's death, I found myself questioning my own life and its meaning. As I moved on without his presence, everything seemed meaningless and confusing. During this time, I thought about how much time on Earth I may have left. Twenty to thirty years ... Wow, I had never thought about my life in this manner before. How quickly this time would likely go by. Somehow this brought my life into perspective. Twenty to thirty years didn't seem long at all. I thought to myself that I better start living and stop putting my dreams and goals off until tomorrow.

How quickly my fears arose. According to Freud, fear of death is universal to the human condition. This certainly didn't bring me any comfort. We all are aware that we will die some day, but that is so far off in the future that we fail to think about that fateful day very much. With the death of someone close, your own demise suddenly seems plausible and real. My fear was pure resistance and wanting to run back to a time when I felt safe. According to Stephen Levine in *A Year to Live*, "Fear leans backward to the last safe moment, while desire leans forward toward the next possibility." My last moment was the day before Dad's death. I needed to stop resisting the inevitable and decide what I wanted or desired the rest of my life to be.

I was not afraid of death, per se, but more of the pain. I was more curious and believe I have always been so since my nursing days. What would happen to me when I died? Where would I go? Somehow the thought of dying brought its own comfort in knowing that I would get to find out!

I knew there was more to us than just a body. Religion talks about a soul and spirit. How do we as humans wrap our minds around these thoughts? They seem so nebulous. Our body dies, but where does our essence go? As part of my nurse training, we junior nurses all had to go to the morgue to see an autopsy being performed. During my visit to the morgue, another student and I accompanied the staff nurse. I walked in and immediately saw on either side of me two wax bodies. "Oh, isn't that perfect? The medical students get to practise first on these wax bodies," I voiced. "No, these aren't made of wax. These are bodies awaiting autopsy," the staff nurse replied. We continued further into the building. We were going to see the autopsy of a patient who had died on our ward. When I saw him, at first I didn't recognize him for he, too, looked like the wax bodies I had just seen. So what was missing? What made them so devoid of their essence? It had gone; the soul, the person's spirit was no longer there. Their eyes when opened were devoid of any human warmth. That was when my fear of death left me and when curiousity and wonder took its place.

It wasn't my fear of dying then that caused my fears. It was my fear of living! When we live our lives in fear, of pleasing others, of thinking only of others, of getting good grades, a good job, marrying well, having children, grandchildren ... these are all phases of life we willingly walk, but at what cost to ourselves? Whose dream have we bought into and where along the way did we lose our own dreams? How can we focus on ourselves, on being authentic and doing what pleases us? How many times have we wanted to do something, go somewhere, have something that would please us, only to realize that we can't afford it? Or worse yet, what if we fail? We sabotage and stop ourselves, contenting ourselves with the next best thing.

I realized that a lot of my life had been spent holding back in fear, but were those fears really mine? I realized that many of them were fears that my father had projected onto me. Whatever controls my dad held over me were now gone. I no longer had to prove anything anymore in order to be validated by him. I was set free. Freedom, which I so relish, was given back to me. But, just like a caged animal remains in the cage even though the door has been opened, I, too, remained with my old self-view, unable to enjoy my new-found freedom and life. I didn't know what I wanted to do now. I had nothing to prove to anyone else, only to myself. It would take time to grow into my new sense of self. First I had to relinquish what I didn't want before I could determine what it was that I did want. I set off to find my purpose as soon as I got my bearings, and my compass stopped spinning and pointed the way. My ascent up the mountain began. For me this was about six months after my dad died. It was through my working with a coach that I became connected to activities I enjoyed and was good at. It would be another year, however, before that job would emerge fully. But at least I had hope and direction. I had energy for the first time in a long time.

3. **We are welcomed back once we have come through the grief**

Grief's Abyss

process. Like all good heroes and sheroes, in search of a quest, we leave our ordinary lives behind when someone we love dies and our journey into grief begins. Some may refuse the call of this adventure, preferring denial instead. As we begin to accept the death and pick up the pieces of our lives, we are tested by our fears, our guilt, and our anger. Once we deal with grief and make friends with our emotions, we can continue our life's journey and start to make sense of our ordeal. With the death of our loved one we get to face our own immortality and fears, and we get to slay the demons that have held us back thus far in life. We get to claim our gift, our treasure in seeing ourselves grow emotionally and, most important of all, we get to live our lives on our terms. The decision to make whatever time we have left on Earth count is made.

We can now rush up the mountain to the very top, for it is now time to celebrate and be welcomed back into life. We can proudly show our treasure, the map we clutch tightly in our hands. We have been through Grief's Abyss and we have found our way out of it. We now have the tools to cope. We have been on our own vision quest and have survived it. Come, let's go and be welcomed back by our tribe, our community, and our ancestors. Our initiation is now complete.

CYCLES OF LIFE

SO OUR LIFE continues; the chaos has been left behind; and our wheel turns slowly. This time we are moving upward and like all cycles, the wheel will continue to move its position and, with it, our lives. How many times have you viewed your life with its multiple highs and lows? Nature shows us how timeless the cycles of nature are, birth, life and death, or The Wheel of Samsara. Buddha was the one who described Samsara and the complete cycle of cause and effect. Samsara is not an actual world or life, but it is how we perceive our world to be. The root of suffering in this wheel comes from passion, aggression, and delusion.

It seems we have to understand and move through each one to evolve into a higher, more enlightened state. Remember the movie, *Groundhog Day*, where the hero's day keeps repeating itself until he gets everything right? What if our lives were like that? We are born and then we die to each life, and then come back again to get it right.

There is also the Wheel of Fortune, an ancient pagan divinatory tool from the Tarot pack. In it, we see a picture of three women: the youngest one is spinning; a more mature woman is measuring; and an old woman is cutting. These women are the Moirai from Greek mythology and together they spin a human life into being. They are the goddesses of Fate. The length of a person's life and the time of death are woven into their thread. The Wheel of Fortune is not good or bad, and is not about sudden turns of luck, chance, or accident. There is an intelligent plan at work with it, not a random one. It is in these moments where we can blame fate, luck, or others for the misfortunes that befall us. We would never notice the ups in life if not for the downs. For it is in these low moments that we have the greatest opportunities for growth. It is when life or Fate shakes us up and out of our complacency that we come to terms with our destiny. If we do not learn from these hard times, then history will repeat itself and our lives end up like Groundhog Day.

According to S.L. Scott, fate is the life you lead if you never put yourself in the path of greatness. Destiny is your potential waiting to happen ... WHY settle for an ordinary life?

Whatever we do or don't do in our lives, it's important to realize that we have an impact in some way on the lives of others. By our being on Earth, we cannot avoid affecting others. It may be a smile to help someone get through the day. It might be a best-selling novel we write that helps thousands of other people cultivate happier lives. Whatever path you choose, it is critical you know that you matter and so does your life. I, like you, will leave my influence on Earth when I die. Those who I have touched and affected, those who have been helped in some way by my presence, I will never know ... but this is my legacy. It gives me great joy to know my life mattered.

Grief, they say, does not have an end. As with all cycles of life, grief

Grief's Abyss

recedes and waits for the wheel to turn again and for its call to return. When it does come back, hopefully you won't be quite so afraid because you will know what to expect. Grief is a part of life and to love another being means risking its pain. We know when our loved ones die, our grief will be great and we will mourn.

The cycle is complete; we are back on the road to life. Will Grief's Abyss be the same when it is time for you to return to it?

REFLECTIONS

1. How will you reconnect with hope and joy?

Hope is the engine that keeps us moving forward. If we had no hope, how would we survive? We are always hoping for a better outcome or a better day. Make a list of all the things you are hoping for.

What brings you joy? It doesn't have to be big; it can be joy in the smallest of things—a baby's smile, a touch, a sunset. Joy is always bubbling under the surface. We just need to scratch the surface to release it.

2. How has grief isolated you and what have you learned from this experience?

Just as the Native American young boy is isolated from the world he has known when he leaves to go on his vision quest, grief, too, forces us all on our own vision quest. That young boy has to rely on his own skills and find courage to continue. He faces his fears and conquers them. And in so doing, he grows into a man, realizes his own power, and can then return to his village a wiser soul.

Make a list in your journal of all the things that you have had to face and what you have conquered.

3. How have you faced your own immortality?

Stephen Levine in his book, A Year to Live, writes that it is only in learning how to die, to release all our attachments, and face our fears of the unknown that we can truly live. The death of a loved one forces us to face our own death. What steps have you taken to face yours?

RECOMMENDED RESOURCES

A GPS for Grief and Healing. *3 Powerful Steps to Help You Move from Mourning to Morning.* Rabbi Mel Glazer

A Time to Grieve. *Meditations for Healing After the Death of a Loved One.* Carol Staudacher

A Year to Live. *How to Live This Year as if it Were Your Last.* Stephen Levine

Baby Boomers Face Grief. *Survival and Recovery.* Jane Galbraith

Body Mind Balancing. *Using Your Mind to Heal Your Body.* Osho

Comfortable With Uncertainty. *108 Teachings on Cultivating Fearlessness and Compassion.* Pema Chodron

Healing Grief, Finding Peace. *101 Ways to Cope With the Death of Your Loved One.* Dr. Louis E. Lagrand

Helping Grieving People. *When Tears Are Not Enough.* J. Shep Jeffreys

I Can't Stop Crying: Grief and Recovery, A Compassionate Guide. John D. Martin & Frank D. Ferris

I Thought It Was Just Me. **Making the Journey From "What Will People Think?" to "I Am Enough."** Brené Brown, PhD., LMSW

I Wasn't Ready to Say Goodbye. **Surviving, Coping & Healing After the Sudden Death of a Loved One.** Brook Noel & Pamela D. Blair Ph.D.

Inspiration in Action. *A Woman's Guide to Happiness.* Kathie Donovan

Life After Loss. *A practical guide to renewing your life after experiencing major loss.* Bob Deits

Loving What Is. *Four Questions That Can Change Your Life.* Byron Katie

On Life After Death. Elisabeth Kubler-Ross

Power vs Force. The Hidden Determinants of Human Behavior. David Hawkins, M.D., Ph.D

The Astonishing Power of Emotions. Let Your Feelings Be Your Guide. Esther & Jerry Hicks

The Awakening Course. The Secret to Solving All Problems. Joe Vatale

The End of Your Life Book Club. Will Schwalbe

The Grief Recovery Handbook. The Action Program for Moving Beyond Death, Divorce and Other Losses, Including Health, Career, and Faith. York. John W. James & Russell Friedman

The Happiness Project. Or, Why I Spent a Year Trying to Sing in the Morning, Clean My Closets, Fight Right, Read Aristotle, and Generally Have More Fun. Gretchen Rubin

The Healing Wisdom of Africa. Finding Life Purpose through Nature, Ritual and Community. Malidoma Patrice Somé

The Hope. A Guide to Sacred Activism. Andrew Harvey

The Language of Emotions. What Your Feelings Are Trying to Tell You. Karla McLaren

The not so big life making room for what really matters. Sarah Susanka

The Other Side of Sadness. What the New Science of Bereavement Tells Us About Life After Loss. George A. Bonanno

The Power of Now. A Guide to Spiritual Enlightenment. Eckhart Tolle

The Ten Things to Do When Life Falls Apart. An Emotional and Spiritual Handbook. Daphne Rose Kingma

There's a Spiritual Solution to Every Problem. Wayne W. Dyer

Transcending Loss. Understanding the Lifelong Impact of Grief and How to Make It Meaningful. Ashley Davis Bush

Grief's Abyss

Understanding Your Grief. Ten Essential Touchstones for Finding Hope and Healing Your Heart. Alan D. Wolfelt

You Can Heal Your Heart. Finding Peace After a Breakup, Divorce, or Death. Louise L. Hay & David Kessler

You Can Heal Your Life. Louise L. Hay

You'll Get Over It. The Rage of Bereavement. Virginia Ironside

BEREAVEMENT AND SUPPORT IN CANADA

Good Grief - Apple Newsletter - Alberta
www.Albertahealthservices.ca

BC Funeral Association, Bereavement Resource & BC Helpline
www.bcfunerals.com

What to Do Now a Resource Guide - Nova Scotia
www.nsnet.org/bereaved

Counselling Service in Ottawa and Surrounding Areas
www.CapitalChoiceCounselling.com

Centre for Grief and Healing - Toronto
www.bereavedfamilies.ca

Grief & Loss Counselling and Bereavement Service Newfoundland & Labrador/Saskatchewan/NW Territories
www.theravive.com

USA

Grief Haven.org - USA

Facts About Loss and Grief
www.Reachout.com

Centre for Loss and Life Transition
www.Centerforloss.com
http://GriefNet.org - Grace Happens

U.K

Connecting you with Professional support
www.counselling-directory.org.uk

WEBSITES THAT HELP WITH GRIEF AND BEREAVEMENT

(Note: There are many websites. I have included these two only to start you on your research):

115 Helpful Websites on Grief & Bereavement
www.MastersInCounseling.org

64 Things I Wish Someone Had Said
www.whatsyourgrief.com

ACKNOWLEDGEMENTS

AS MANY AN AUTHOR KNOWS, their book wouldn't become possible if it weren't for the dedication of the many wonderful people who supported them along the way. It is with special appreciation and gratitude to Aurora Winters, the founder of the Grief Coach Academy for planting the seed and believing in me and this book. She has been by my side for a year supporting, guiding and leading me on towards my dreams.

I am so grateful to have Lynne Klippel, my editor and mentor, who took me through the painful process of authoring a book. Her calls were invaluable. Through her, I had access to an amazing team of professionals, and it is due to them that this book became a reality. There were many times when I did not feel it would be possible to complete this book, but Lynne and her team got me across the finish line.

My husband Ray gave me loving support and space to create and write. Ray provided meals and shouldered many of the responsibilities around the house while I was writing. He was my first editor and diligently reviewed many re-writes, all without complaint. Our children, Jeff, Kaye, Mike, and Bradley, helped me to believe my dream of writing was possible. Many thanks to you, my beautiful family.

I also have to thank my dear friends for all their encouragement and interest in the book as well as patiently waiting for me to emerge from my office.

Many thanks to my new friends and coaches from the Grief Coach Academy for supplying me with ideas (Book Titles). Without your ongoing support and coaching through Heartbreak to Happiness - I probably would have just been golfing and reading! Everyone of you became my cheerleaders.

I would be remiss if I didn't mention John Eggan, Publisher, Mission Publishing and his team from The Leading Mentors Publishing and Marketing Program. John is a powerhouse of knowledge and through this program I have learnt so much about authoring, publishing and marketing a book. He provided a treasure trove of information. I so appreciate his support in the early days of this project. I also have access to some amazing coaches who both have walked with me through the twists and turns of authoring. Without their guidance many a deadline and committment may have come and gone!

It certainly takes a village to raise a child; it took as you can see an entire village, of talented knowledgeable and professional people; an entire team of support to bring a book to market. It is with gratitude and thanks to everyone in my life over the past year that my dream to author a book has now come true.

ABOUT THE AUTHOR

ANNE E. DEBUTTE is a Heartbreak to Happiness Coach, author, and trained nurse. She retired two years ago from a 32-year career in healthcare. It only took four days of retirement before she decided to restart her career, this time as a coach and author. The year before, her father had died, so she certainly can relate to the pain of losing a parent. It was this experience that made her realize that if this could happen to her, a former nurse, others too would need help coping through grief. She now dedicates her life to helping women move through their grief to reconnect them with their lives. With her help, they can get back to being productive at work and at home and rediscover their purpose and legacy.

Anne has always had an interest in helping others; it is this drive that has led her to want to become a social entrepreneur and philanthropist. A trust fund has been set up and 10% of all revenues from *Grief's Abyss* and from Anne's coaching activities will be given to the fund. In this way, she can continue to give on behalf of Reconnect from Grief, her coaching company.

When Anne isn't at her desk coaching or writing, she can be found on the golf course in the summer or curled up with a good book in front of the fire in winter. Yoga and running help her live a balanced life. Anne lives in Ottawa with her husband, and between them, they have four wonderful adult children.

RECONNECT FROM GRIEF COACHING SERVICES

RECONNECT FROM GRIEF is a coaching service to assist and guide you to redefine your grief experience so you re-emerge from your pain and heartache after loss. As a certified Heartbreak to Happiness® Grief Coach, Anne is able to guide you through a nine-step process that will reconnect you to your life, love and laughter. There are a variety of coaching packages available to help you.

To determine if coaching is right for you, please go to www.reconnect-from-grief.com and register for a complimentary discovery session "Finding your Pathway to Peace"

For more information please contact:

www.Reconnect-From-Grief.com
Reconnect-from-Grief
5588 Main Street
Manotick, ON
K4M 1B3
1-613-979-2418

You may also email Anne at: anne@reconnect-from-grief.com

As a special gift for readers Anne has prepared an audio of her Poem "The Journey" (featured at the beginning of the book) which has been set to music.

This can be obtained by going to:
http://www.reconnect-from-grief.com/readergift/

www.ingramcontent.com/pod-product-compliance
Lightning Source LLC
Chambersburg PA
CBHW071721090426
42738CB00009B/1843